W9-BCT-715

God's Armor

Bellwether

Mother Nadine

Intercessors of the Lamb
Omaha, NE

Nihil obstat
Reverend Michael F. Gutgsell, J.C.L.
Chancellor

Imprimatur
+Most Reverend Elden Francis Curtiss
Archbishop of Omaha
May 15, 1999

Copyright ©1998 by Intercessors of the Lamb.

First printing: September 1998
Second printing: November 2002

Additional copies of this book may be obtained through our
web page store or by contacting:

Intercessors of the Lamb
4014 North Post Road
Omaha, NE 68112
e-mail: bellwether@novia.net
web page: www.bellwetheromaha.org

Published in the United States.

Library of Congress Catalog Card Number: 98-72294
ISBN: 0-9664956-0-8

All rights reserved. No part of this book may be reproduced
or transmitted in any form without the written permission
of the publisher.

God's Armor

"Put on the armor of God
so that you may be able to stand firm
against the tactics of the devil."
Eph 6:11

"Draw your strength from the Lord
and from his mighty power.
Put on the armor of God so that
you may be able to stand firm
against the tactics of the devil.
Our battle is not against human forces
but against the principalities and powers,
the rulers of this world of darkness,
the evil spirits in the regions above.
You must put on the armor of God,
if you are to resist on the evil day;
do all that your duty requires
and hold your ground.
Stand fast, with the truth as the belt
around your waist,
justice as your breastplate,
and zeal to propagate
the gospel of peace as your footgear.
In all circumstances,
hold faith up before you as your shield;
it will help you extinguish
the fiery darts of the evil one.
Take the helmet of salvation
and the sword of the Spirit,
the word of God.
At every opportunity, pray in the Spirit,
using prayers and petitions of every sort.
Pray constantly and attentively
for all in the holy company."
Eph 6:10-18

Preface

Mankind is currently in the midst of a spiritual war. There's no getting around it. Evil rises around us as never before. Witchcraft is now practiced in the open, children are killing children, and vulgarity dominates the popular culture. Technology is the new god, and we hear of New Age infiltration everywhere from the classroom to the White House.

In the current spiritual maelstrom, in the challenges of such an era, in the danger of demonism, there can be no more important book than the one you now hold in your hands. It is written by one of the foremost experts in spiritual intercession, Mother Nadine, and it comes to us as a light that splits the current dark. It is not just a book about evil, but more than that it is a book about how we can defend ourselves against demonic onslaughts—how we can protect ourselves and loved ones—and how, with Christ, we can transcend evil.

It's a book about spiritual warfare, but more than that it is a book about spiritual development, one that every Catholic should read, a book full of information that should be preached from the pulpit. As Mother Nadine knows only too well, the urgent task in our time is to arm ourselves against the assaults of Satan. He prowls like a roaring lion. He is the master deceiver. He attacks constantly. It is crucial that we learn how to defend ourselves. It's crucial to realize that life on earth is a constant test, and we must get by the evil snares before we find our way to paradise.

That's what this book is about: protecting against evil and defeating it, winning at spiritual warfare. Across the spiritual landscape is evidence that evil is rising to a frightening degree and must be confronted. Materialism, greed, and lust have all but obscured the nobler aspirations of life as demons harass the children of God. Everywhere are accounts of infestation. In suburbs of New York City, children play demonic games and actually call out to spirits to possess them. In San Francisco, city officials attend a party at which satanic rituals are performed. In Hollywood are rampant paganism and impurity.

We must confront such evil, and we must purge it, or God will purge it for us. In this book, Mother Nadine gives a tremendously insightful glimpse into the workings of evil and tells us how to rid its onset. She tells us where it is. She explains how it takes root. She describes the characteristics of evil and carefully delineates the way to get it out of our lives.

Let me repeat that Mother Nadine and her new community of Intercessors in Omaha, Nebraska, are a shining light in a world of darkness. They are true prayer warriors. They have set upon an exciting course that dispels falsity with truth and darkness with love. They don't conduct their deliverance with flamboyance. They don't scream and shout. Instead, they go about purging evil with the key components of Christianity: faith, humility, and love. They are biblical. They are careful to follow the Church's teachings. As I said, Mother Nadine is one of our country's foremost experts on spiritual warfare, and her insights and wisdom will never be forgotten by those who take the time to read her work.

In this book you'll get a feeling of how to transcend the evil all around you and begin taking measures to protect your families. Who better to instruct us than Mother Nadine? I've known her for years, and I have been constantly impressed by her strength and fearlessness. She is one of God's very special warriors, and she employs the best tools of both charismatic and Marian devotions in ridding evil from people's lives.

Please read this book slowly. Please read it carefully. And please pass it on.

It is a book of wisdom. It is a book of crucial knowledge. It is a blueprint for victory. And it is filled with something the devil can never conquer: Christ's sweet and humble love.

Michael H. Brown
September 1988

Chapter 1

God's Armor

"Put on the armor of God
so that you may be able to stand firm
against the tactics of the devil."
Eph 6:11

Several years ago one of the sisters and I were visiting Colorado, and we decided to visit a Trappist Monastery at Snowmass. It didn't look very far on the map, but by the time we got into that area it was dark. We were in the mountains, and we didn't know our way around. We thought that we had better turn around and go back, but as we studied the map a little further, we thought, "Well, here's a shortcut." Well, let me tell you, there are no shortcuts in the mountains! And there are no shortcuts to God, either.

Anyway, we took the shortcut. It took us over a dangerous pass, and we saw that the road was getting narrower and narrower. I was in the passenger seat, and I could just look straight down over the edge of the mountain, and I thought, "Oh my! Oh my!" Finally, there was a little curve around a tree, and we decided to pull off here and somehow turn around. It was too dangerous to continue on. We pulled off and were sitting there getting our bearings with our map, when a car with several men in it pulled in front to block us. We both could feel evil, and so I said, "You don't even have time to turn around; they're blocking us. Just step on the gas, and we'll have to keep going." We knew we were in danger.

They took off right after us, and so I started praying for help. It was a beautiful feast day of Our Lady, so my thoughts were on her, and I asked her to help us, too. The evil seemed to get worse, and we needed help now! So I called on the Lord, "Lord, save us. We're perishing." Then it started to rain! It was getting dark, we're going over one of the highest passes in the Rockies, and it's thundering and lightning. We were practically hugging the mountain, just inching our way to stay on the road. This other car was right behind us, full of evil. It was like we didn't have any control, and both of us knew it.

I said, "Maybe, since nobody's hearing us up there, we'd better make an Act of Contrition. I think we might be going." So we did. You could just feel the clamminess and the coldness of evil, and then all of a sudden I thought, "What am I thinking of? The one Person I trust more than anyone is the Father." This is how Jesus taught us to pray, "Father, deliver us from the evil one" (Mt 6:13). So that's how we prayed, one sentence, "Father, deliver us from this evil!" Instantly it lifted. Instantly! The car behind us got further and further back, and we came out of it. What a powerful way to teach us that there is an evil that the Father has to come against Himself in order to rescue us. Jesus knew this.

The prayer of a warrior is really the prayer Jesus taught us, the Our Father. The focus of the prayer of a warrior is particularly the part, "Deliver us from evil" (Mt 6:13). Some translations say, "Deliver us from the evil one." When we give a face to evil and refer to it as the evil one, we are alerted that this evil is a power that is active, not just a nebulous concept. When we say the evil one, we mean that there's a personality here. The evil one is a spirit with a specific mission of his very own; there's no doubt about it.

The contemplative John could see in a special way because he had the vision of eagles. Through the wisdom gift, contemplatives see through God's eyes because they have listening hearts. John's wisdom didn't come through his mind or from books, but it proceeded from his Heart-to-heart communication with Jesus. John "leaned back against Jesus' chest" (Jn 13:25), and it was here that he learned, straight from Jesus' heart. John could see this evil even back then, "The whole world is under the evil one" (1 Jn 5:19). John knew the power the evil one had. He also knew that this evil one is a personality, a real, live, active being, and not just a concept. Today we can see that the whole world is still very much under the power of the evil one, and we must go to the Father to deliver us from him.

Jesus taught us how to do this. As He went to the Father to be delivered from evil, we, too, are to go to the Father to be delivered from this evil one. The Father has the power to deliver us, and He wants us to share in this power. In 1 John 4:4 we are reminded of this: "For there is One greater *in you* than there is in the world." Now satan knows very well that because of our relationship with Father, we have access to Him and His power. We are the ones who tend to forget there is One greater *within* us. The greatest power that we have is the Father and our relationship with Him. Our number one weapon for spiritual warfare is our Abba, our Daddy. It's beautiful!

Therefore, our relationship with the Father is key. It is very important to have a relationship with the Father, particularly for prayer warriors; we need a relationship like Jesus had with His Father. Of course this relationship will develop and deepen as we grow more and more into union with Jesus. This relationship is important so that when we're praying, we're not just reciting a prayer. Rather, we are asking Someone we know personally, Someone we belong to, Someone who is our Daddy, to deliver us from evil. This is essential.

You might know about my own little experience of how I met the Father. Hindsight is always 20/20; we can always see really well in retrospect. When I was studying to become a member of the Catholic Church in my early twenties, I did not tell my own father that I was taking instructions because I knew he wouldn't be very happy about it. I wanted the instructions to go along smoothly so I thought, "I won't tell him now. When I'm baptized into the Catholic Church, then I'll tell him, and it'll be okay." Daddy and I were very, very close. My mother had died, and my father had remarried and was no longer living in Omaha. So I was baptized Christmas Eve, and the next day, Christmas Day, he and his wife came to town. I told them, "Oh, guess what?" Well, it was a disaster! It was a total disaster. In fact, he disowned me. I was deeply hurt because I'm the only girl, and daughters and fathers have a special kind of relationship many times. He not only disowned me, but when he got back home, he put it in writing. I was very, very upset about this.

I was so hurt that I sat down in a very childish way and wrote a letter that one would think was written by a teenager. "Well, if you're not going to be my father anymore then I'm not going to be your daughter." It was that kind of letter, but I took it to the priest who had instructed me. This was kind of interesting. Why I ever did that I really don't know because in the past I had never shown a letter to anybody before I sent it, but for some reason I took it to this priest. He sat there on the other side of the desk. He read my reply, and he shook his head very, very slowly, like "No, we don't do this." I sat on the other side of the desk and said, "What do you mean, we don't do this?" He said, "Well, I mean we turn the other cheek." I said, "Oh, really, who said that?" He said, "Jesus." "Oh, really, what does that mean for me? Translate that." He said, "You've been writing to your father about every two weeks telling him what you're doing and your activities. That means that you continue doing that. It means that you go to Mass every day like you have started to do now as a Catholic, and you pray your heart out." You pray your heart out.

There it was. From my earliest days in the Catholic Church, the Lord was busy preparing me for this type of ministry. He was leading me into intercession right from the very beginning. I didn't understand it at the time, but now I can see clearly why this happened. My first couple months in the Catholic Church were spent in deep prayer for my father. It never entered my mind to pray for myself. I was just driven to pray for my father so that he could understand me and my actions. After three months of intense prayer, he had a wonderful dream. His father, who is my grandfather and who is not living, came to him and said, "It's all right. She's a child of God's now."

This is truly what was happening to me in those three months. I was raised with a very close relationship with my earthly father and now that we were separated, I desperately needed a father in my life. This forced me to go to the Father with all my needs right away. I had not ever lived without a father, so I came into relationship with the Heavenly Father right then. It's a beautiful relationship that grows deeper each day and hopefully will always grow.

I urge all of you to work at developing your relationship with the Father. Many of you might already have a relationship with the Father, but if you don't, it's a special gift that I encourage you to ask for. It is pure gift, but this is the mission of Jesus, isn't it? His whole mission is to take us to the Father. He said, "The Father is greater than I" (Jn 14:28). Jesus is never going to be enough for any of us, particularly for prayer warriors. Towards the end of Jesus' life, Philip, who had been with Jesus for three years, said,

"Lord, show us the Father and that will be enough for us"(Jn 14:8). So our relationship with Jesus will come to a point where it won't be enough. Our relationship with the Father is essential, particularly as we pray to deliver us from this constant evil. God is so powerful, and He has a tremendous strategy!

In Mark 9:14-28 the apostles tried to cast out a demon, and they couldn't do it. When they asked Jesus what they had done wrong, He said, "This kind you can drive out only by prayer." Some Bible translations say, "by prayer and fasting." Did you ever wonder what Jesus meant when He said "this kind"? I used to meditate on that a lot, and I'm sure there are many different theories, but I have come to know in recent years that there is a this kind of evil, and it's very, very high powered. The Father alone is the One who can deliver us from "this kind." In fact, just recently I was praying with somebody via phone who wanted prayer for an estranged member of her family. When we went into prayer, we discovered that this person was involved in such high-powered evil that the Lord told me, "For this kind, you just ask Me to do it. You stay out of it, and leave it to Me. I'll deliver him." The image that came was of the Father coming and lifting him right out of the flames of hell. So that's what I mean; there is a "this kind" of evil, and we need the Father to be the Deliverer.

I didn't always know this, but it's interesting. There is a power in the ministry for "this kind" of spiritual warfare. Not too long ago I was meditating on the Our Father where Jesus said, "Father, deliver us from evil," and it occurred to me that the way the Father chooses to deliver us is through Jesus and His Sacrifice. Jesus **is** the Deliverer. Jesus became a victim of His own intercession. When we pray, we do, too. We sometimes become the "victim" of our own prayers. Many times after asking God to do something, it seems like our whole life starts to fall apart. We wonder, "My God, where are You?" He's right there, probably answering our prayers but now we have become the victim lambs of our own intercession. He is asking us to carry part of the burden. He is using our sacrifice to make up for the lack of love. It's powerful. Jesus became the very One that would be the answer to the prayer, "Father, deliver us from evil." The Father answered the prayer, "I will deliver you from evil, and it will be through You, My Son." Now, through Jesus living in us, His Body here on the earth, we, too, will be victims of our own intercession.

When we're involved in this kind of ministry, the evil can seem so overwhelming at times. If we're not careful, we can have the tendency to take on the burdens ourselves and try to bring about the answers to these prayers through our own actions. This is why we constantly have to come back to this relationship with the Father and let Him be in charge. This is how we stay little. We take it to the Lord; here we can rest. In our humanity we can get our focus off God like poor Peter. He was walking on the water, but then he took his eyes off Jesus and began to sink (see Mt 14:28-33). This can happen to us, too, and everything will seem to go wrong; the washing machine overflows, the kids are fighting, and your appliances and cars break down all at once. There is always going to be that last straw that breaks our backs, and we cry out, "Oh, Lord, where are You?" Then we can start to sink if we're not careful.

I must have been at this sinking spot a few weeks ago, when I had an image of St. Michael. He's big in this image, like a Paul Bunyan-type big. He's huge and is in full armor. I was in the image, too, and I came up to his kneecap! He said, "You're little. Remember, Nadine, you're little, and the battle belongs to the Lord." I want to pass that on to you. We're little; we're just little ones, thank goodness. It is in our littleness and weaknesses that we are strong (see 2 Cor 12:10). When we're little, we draw on the strength of the Lord, and the battle **is** the

Lord's. We sometimes forget this because we tend to get so involved in whatever we're doing, but we need to remember that the battle is the Lord's. There is strength in knowing that we're never alone; the Lord is always with us. He is also calling forth other prayer warriors, so we are never alone.

St. Michael is a very close and dear friend of prayer warriors. We don't do anything without St. Michael the Archangel. If you don't know St. Michael personally, hopefully you will come to know him soon. When I was taking instructions to join the Catholic Church, the priest happened to mention this angel, St. Michael the Archangel. I had never heard of him. In fact, I hadn't ever met anyone with the name Michael before. I remember sitting there saying to this priest, "This is the first Michael I've ever met. I think we're going to be good friends." Well, how little did I know just how good!

The New Age movement is in the Church, although it is not being spotted as such. Popes have written about it, warning of its inherent dangers to our Church and us. In 1907, a beautiful Encyclical by Pope Pius X, *Syllabus Condemning the Errors of the Modernists* came out, calling this New Age movement modernism. But we never heard anything more about it or what we should do to prevent it. The prophetic warning fell by the wayside. Pius XII was very concerned that this modernism, this New Age movement, would creep into the Church, and it has. It comes in under the guise of prayer; it comes in through false contemplative prayer and false mysticism.

Pope John Paul II, as Karol Cardinal Wojtyla, also tried to warn us back in 1976 of the terrible effect the evil one would have on our society and Church. He said,

> "We are now standing in the face of the greatest historical confrontation humanity has gone through. I do not think that wide circles of American society or wide circles

18

of Christian community realize this fully. We are now facing the final confrontation between the Church and the anti-church, the Gospel versus the anti-gospel. This confrontation lies within the plan of divine Providence; it is a trial which the whole Church must take up" ("Notable & Quotable", Karol Cardinal Wojtyla, *Wall Street Journal*, Nov. 9, 1978).

Pope John Paul II has spoken a great deal about this evil. He is a very prophetic pope, and in much of what he has said we can see the vision he has of what is coming to the Church. We can see that this trial has begun; we are at war.

This trial that is here really shouldn't surprise us because when we read Genesis, particularly Genesis 3:15, we see that it was God who declared war. He said, "I will put enmity between you and the woman, and between your offspring and hers; He will strike at your head, while you strike at his heel." The Heavenly Father is the aggressor here. He took the initiative and declared war against satan. This trial isn't something that we have to be fearful of, as if satan were in charge and the one who declared war. No, it is the Father who declared war. We, too, are involved in this battle because we're part of the Body of Christ. We belong in prayer with Our Lady. Did you know she has her combat boots on? She's gathering her prayer warriors. She's visiting all over the world today, one apparition after another. It's just amazing!

I like to recall one of the times when we were in Medjugorje and one of the priests who was with us did not have his homily ready. He had the privilege of being one of the main celebrants for the big Mass in St. James. This is really an honor for a priest so he wanted it to be a very special homily, but his homily didn't come. It didn't come, and all the way over in the plane he thought, "She'll give it to me when we get to Medjugorje. She'll give it to me then." So now we're in Medjugorje, it's 9 a.m., and he still doesn't have it. The American-English liturgy will be starting at 10 o'clock, he still doesn't have his homily ready, and he's really getting nervous. Priests are starting to pile into the sacristy to get vested. So he found a little, tiny spot in the sacristy where nobody was around, right in front of a statue of St. Joseph. So he said, "Joseph, she's not answering me. Please ask your spouse to give me the homily. It's just 30 minutes away." There was a silence, and he could have sworn he heard St. Joseph say, "I can't do that. She's never home anymore!" So she's a lady on the move, isn't she? She's never home anymore! She's right here with us, gathering us together and forming us for what lies ahead.

One day I heard all this commotion in our backyard. It had a different cry, like a bird in distress, so I went out to the backyard to see what was happening. As I looked up into a tree, there was a big snake trying to get to the bird's nest to get her eggs. I had never seen a snake face to face before. Now for a person in spiritual warfare you'd think that wouldn't bother me, but as some of you know, when I was in the cloister I was the only nun that had permission to wear garden gloves because I was afraid I'd touch a worm! I'm about the last one God should have called into this.

Anyway, I saw this snake, which is symbolic for satan and evil, and I thought, "Oh my goodness. I can't let this snake get these little eggs." So I ran into the house to get a broomstick, and when I came out, the snake saw me coming. He didn't even slither down the tree. He just literally dropped. He just dropped. He couldn't get away fast enough. The eggs were safe. Later I thought about this. Nothing happens by chance, nothing. As I pondered about this situation, there was a deep teaching in there for me. What the Lord was showing me was first, when He wants me to confront evil, when it's *in His time*, there will

20

be no fear in confrontation. No matter what the evil is or how high powered it is, there will be no fear at all.

We see this in the natural life, too. We hear about mothers throwing themselves in front of bears to save their child or having the strength to lift a car to rescue their child. Love is so powerful! It has a strength beyond that of the people themselves. They don't even think of themselves, and it will be the same when we move against high-powered evil. God's love will overcome us and completely take over the situation. God's love is so powerful, it conquers all!

The other thing the Lord showed me in this little incident was that satan is trying to rob life today in the womb. He's trying to prevent life from reaching its potential. He's trying to take life from the eggs even before they're hatched, as we're seeing in the alarming number of abortions today. He's trying to rob teenagers of their full potential. He's even trying to destroy life in those of us who are walking with the Lord through busyness and the spirit of the world that can rob us of our time to pray everyday. Satan is always trying to rob. He's a thief; he steals what doesn't belong to him. This whole movement of evil that's going through the world today has many faces, but the bottom line is that it's the same mover behind it all. It's the same Lucifer behind it. We must always remember that the battle belongs to the Lord, and it will be okay. God is more powerful, and He has a tremendous strategy.

So **"Put on the armor of God so that you may be able to stand firm against the tactics of the devil"** (Eph 6:11). We know that we have already won because the victory has already been won by Jesus, and truly the battle *is* the Lord's!

Chapter 2

The Belt of Truth

"Stand fast, with. . . the truth as the belt around your waist."
Eph 6:14

Everything in our world changes. People don't keep their word today. Even our parents might not have kept their word to us: such as, "If you go to sleep and be a good little girl, I'll see that you get some candy in the morning." Well, morning came, it was the seventh day, and our parents rested! We grow up with an attitude of questioning whatever we hear: maybe it's true, maybe it's not true. This is not all bad because this forces us into discerning and seeking out what is true and what isn't.

But just what is truth? When we hear the word truth, what do we think? Do we think of mere facts? As Christians, we cannot speak of truth in these terms; we must speak of the Holy Spirit, the Spirit of Truth. This is what truth means. The Holy Spirit is Truth Himself, and He lives within us as He lived in Jesus. Jesus said, "I am the way and the truth"(Jn 14:6). Today more than ever we need the Holy Spirit, the Belt of Truth.

Imagine going off to war in full armor and forgetting our belts. It wouldn't work. We'd be tripping all over, dropping parts of our armor, stumbling. The belt holds everything together. If we are to be used as God's prayer warriors, we must have on the belt of truth, the Holy Spirit. Without the Holy Spirit, the armor will not be effective or stay in place.

We may be concerned now, wondering, "How can we get the Holy Spirit as our belt of truth? We're not so wise, We're just little." And this is exactly how. We are little, and when we're little, we need the Holy Spirit to be in charge totally. Consider Jesus' words, "I assure you, unless you change and become like little children, you will not enter the kingdom of God" (Mt 18:3). Children always check everything out. They ask question after question. Children know that they need help. This does not mean that we do not use our intellect, but rather it means that we know that we need the Holy Spirit to be in charge.

So in order to remain in truth, we must be walking forward in truth ourselves. Discernment is knowing the difference between light and darkness, truth and deception, love and fear, and good and evil. It is knowing the difference between the two leaders, Jesus and satan. Discernment means we check everything out with the Holy Spirit who is active within us. We need His help. Hopefully the Holy Spirit will keep us aware that He is our helper so we will always check things out with Him first.

We need to learn about truth because we are constantly dealing with untruth and deception. Jesus called satan a liar (see Jn 8:44). But how do we know what is true or untrue unless we are walking forward in truth ourselves? We may not even know it's getting dark unless we are living in the light. We may not even be aware that the air is getting more and more polluted. It's a gradual thing, and it can catch us off guard. We need discernment in this age where truth and untruth can easily get mixed up.

It's interesting that it wasn't until after the Charismatic Renewal began in the Catholic Church that this whole concept of evil began coming more into the light. All of a sudden we became more aware of things around us, and even within us, that we just weren't aware of before. It's like He, the Spirit of Truth, almost didn't exist before. We never spotted deception or evil. Then all of a sudden, with the coming of the Holy Spirit and His Light, we started to see deception. Now we can see it everywhere today. We can turn on the news and hear it in newscasters, and we can hear it in press releases from our government. Deception is everywhere; maybe it's just in shades, but it's there. This is when our intuitive gift of discernment from the Spirit of Truth Himself comes in. Sometimes the way He lets us know is almost by instinct; we call it an "anointing." It's when something within us says, "Put on the brakes" or like when a cat all of a sudden hunches up. Maybe the cat doesn't know what's out there, but it's on guard. The Spirit may be activated within us, letting us know, "Be careful here. Something just isn't right. Watch it." This is the Spirit of Truth, God's light, being activated within us.

Sometimes we may not trust this intuitive gift of discernment and move against it thinking, "Oh, that's just me." But as we look back, we can see the Holy Spirit is teaching us to be conscious of our intuition, to be obedient to that voice of the Spirit within us. When the heart speaks, we must take time right then to ask Him, "What is going on here? Why am I on guard? Why doesn't this sit right with me?" This warning will not always be alerting us of evil, per se. Sometimes it might be the Father desiring to show us a weak spot within us that needs to be looked at in order to make us more whole. It is very important to become sensitive to the movement of the Spirit within our hearts.

Discernment takes place not so much in the mind but in the heart. The mind takes in the facts. We need the facts for good discernment, but then we have to go into the heart, into the intuitive. The heart has its own logic, and hopefully it will go along with the mind, but many times it will not, so we need to check things out with the Father.

The mind is not in charge. God, who lives deep within our heart, is in charge. We always go into the heart for discernment.

Awhile back, a doctor called me from another state. He had previously separated from another practice because the other doctors were focused on money and were not standing for the things that the Church teaches in medicine. He was wondering whether he should remain within the practice he had just begun. Should he go into practice with some other doctors who were really urging him to join them, or should he bring in a friend that he went to school with that he knew and trusted? What would be our discernment on this matter using our natural sense? We would think to stay away from the group of doctors and go with the friend that he knows and trusts.

It sounds logical, doesn't it? We would think, "Oh, what's there to discern?" But we always must check it out with the Father to find out what He wants. I told the doctor that we would try to get the discernment for him, but we would also ask specifically that God would give it to him as well. When we prayed, we were amazed that the Lord indicated, very strongly, with many confirmations, that he is to go into practice with this other group! This doctor called the next day and said, "It's the strangest thing, but I don't think I'm to go into practice with my friend." Isn't that interesting? One of the doctors in this other group was a non-Christian doctor, and the Lord assured him that the practice would be Christian. It was okay. Now this was totally opposite of what we would have thought using only our natural minds, but it is the heart that is the discerner.

So we always have to ask. We can never assume that we know the answer. We can make mistakes in assumption. The Lord left the options open for this doctor. In discernment, we will always have options because God always lets us choose, using the beautiful gift of our free will. This is the one gift God will not touch. It's up to us;

He allows us to choose. Even though we may make mistakes, He allows us to choose. He took a great risk when He left us this gift because we can misuse it. So this gift of our free will is to choose, choose, choose all the time. Not to choose, not to make decisions, is to make a choice. The fruit that comes forth from the decision is always the sign as to whether or not the decision was right. Good discernment will always bear good fruit.

For those of us who walk with the Lord day after day, we hear His voice and begin to see how He works, particularly in other people, circumstances, and our own lives. We may begin to assume or presume that we know how God will move or act. This is one of the great pitfalls that satan will use against us. Just as married people have to be very careful not to assume that they know what their spouse will think, do, or say, we likewise have to slow down and check things out. We're children of the Light. We have to see. God does not want us to be in the dark, so until we have His light in every situation, we don't move. We don't guess, "Well, I think . . ." We wait until we find out what God wants. We can seek out other people whom we trust, such as a priest, spiritual director, close friend, or spouse. On major decisions we wait for confirmation before we proceed. The One who gives the confirmation on how we should proceed is the Confirmer, the Holy Spirit. We need the strength and light of the Holy Spirit.

Jesus said, "When the Spirit comes, He will prove the world wrong about sin, about justice, about condemnation" (Jn 16:8). This is what we are seeing Him do. We are starting to see sin in so many manifestations, and one of the first places we start to see sin is within ourselves. It's often been said that one of the greatest tricks of satan is to let everyone believe he (satan) doesn't exist. We have to be careful. We may not recognize his activity within ourselves, and he may even be using us as his agent and instrument.

People often think that satan cannot use or fool Christians, but this is not true. Satan used Peter in an attempt to weaken Jesus' resolve to go to the Cross. Peter was chosen; he was a close friend of Jesus. How could this have happened? It's unbelievable, but satan spoke to Jesus directly through Peter, someone loyal to Jesus. "God forbid that any such thing ever happen to You" (Mt 16:22). Now Jesus, being Jesus, spotted it, but maybe we won't. First of all, the Cross isn't that enticing to most of us; we'd rather take a Tylenol! The whole Church kind of runs pell-mell away from the Cross. It's not natural to follow Jesus to Calvary. There's isn't anything natural about Christianity; it's supernatural. Here's the beauty of it: we need a Power beyond our own, we need light beyond our own, we need judgment beyond our own, and we need wisdom beyond our own. We need the Spirit of Truth, the Holy Spirit Himself.

Jesus said, "Anyone committed to the truth hears my voice." Pilate replies, "Truth! What does that mean?" (Jn 18:37-38). The culture we live in today makes it difficult to hear truth and spot deception. There are so many shades of truth. We might hear 50 percent truth, 50 percent falsehood, or 80 percent/20 percent, or 99 percent/1 percent, but if it's not 100 percent truth, it's not God. God does not shade anything. We are so accustomed to hearing truth mixed in with falsehood. We need to have the belt of truth on. We need to be hearing with the wisdom and discernment of the Holy Spirit.

The gift of discernment is the Holy Spirit Himself. He is pure Light. Satan will disguise himself as an angel of light. We Christians like light, we're used to it, but we may not always spot this false angel of light because he's very clever and deceptive. He (satan) will settle for 97 percent truth if he can trick us on the other 3 percent. But the light of God is brighter! We need this light at all times so that we can detect the shadow, so we'll spot the deception. No matter how close it is to truth, we need it to be 100 percent truth. We need to go to the Holy Spirit and ask, "I need light. Is this truth?" Then His gifts will start to become activated within us. The beautiful Isaiah gifts that we received at Confirmation will start to be put into use.

Once I didn't understand that this gift of discernment was part of our weapons. I didn't even know we were in a battle. But this belt of truth is part of the armor of God, and it is to be used in spiritual warfare. Many in the Church today do not even know there's a spiritual war going on. Once upon a time we could go to Church and never question anything we heard from the pulpit. Well, we can't do that anymore. We can't even read a Catholic newspaper without discerning whether or not this is truth. There's been such an infiltration of deception into the Church by the spirit of the world and by satanic powers. These discerning gifts of the Holy Spirit are beginning to get activated now when we need them the most.

Whenever we're operating in the light, one of the gifts that is activated within us that we all received at Confirmation is the gift of Understanding. Have you ever started to understand something and said, "Oh, now I see." There's a light that goes on. When this understanding comes, we *know* it. It's like someone turned on a light in a dark room, and we can finally see. We are very aware that this light is coming from outside of ourselves. It is not something we made up, and firm conviction accompanies it. It is the light of the Holy Spirit.

The gift of Knowledge is activated tremendously when that light comes on because then we begin to *know*, we begin to know something that we didn't understand before. This is important because in discernment there are always three spirits operating. There is the Holy Spirit, the Spirit of Truth; then there's the evil spirit, the deceiver, the liar; and then there's our spirit, our poor, little, weak, human spirit. Our human spirit is going to adhere either to the

28

Holy Spirit or to the evil spirit. This is why Jesus said, "He who is not with Me, is against Me. He who does not gather with Me scatters" (Mt 12:30).

Jesus is telling us that we have to be totally for Him, or we are against Him. There isn't any compromise in war. We can't straddle the fence. There are no gray areas here. We have to come into His knowledge or we will be stumbling in the dark. We only take the next step when we have the light to take that step. This is extremely important.

Satan is going to pop up throughout this book because there's always the contrast between light and darkness. This helps us to see and spot deception more clearly. I'm quoting Jesus when I say that satan is a liar. Revelation 12:9 refers to him as the one "who deceived the whole world." He's called the deceiver; he's called Lucifer. We probably think of him more as Lucifer because that is the name that he had as the angel of light before the Fall.

"How have you fallen from the heavens, O morning star, son of the dawn" (Is 14:12). Lucifer wanted to be the Morning Star. In the book of Revelation, the very last verses talk about Jesus as the Morning Star. In somewhat of a sarcastic way, God is speaking to Lucifer, "How have you fallen from the heavens, O morning star, son of the dawn! How are you cut down to the ground, you who mowed down the nations! You said in your heart, 'I will scale the heavens; above the stars of God, I will set up my throne; I will take my seat on the Mount of Assembly, in the recesses of the North. I will ascend above the tops of the clouds; I will be like the Most High.' " God replied, "Yet down to the nether world you go, to the recesses of the pit!" (Is 14:12-15)

So we see his fall, but he's not chained. He's roaming. He's very active. When he fell, he took quite a few others with him. We read in Scripture about war breaking out in heaven against St. Michael and his angels. "It's tail (the serpent's) swept away a third of the stars" (Rv 12:4). We're quite certain that at least a third of the angels went with Lucifer—by their choice. It's hard to believe that they would leave by their choice! It's nice to know there are more angels left in heaven, two-thirds anyway! We also have the Trinity, Our Lady, and all the saints standing with us on our side, so we have ample help, believe me.

Let's take a look at how satan works. I'll be quoting from Genesis 3 because satan rarely changes his tactics, particularly because they're so successful. The generation might change, the country might change, the faces of the people might change, but he doesn't change that much. He is a destroyer. His activity will always destroy. His activity can even murder, as we see in the story of Cain and Abel.

One of satan's main tools is division. We might not spot division as easily as some of his other tools because sometimes division isn't that destructive in the early stage. Satan doesn't care how long he has to wait. He'll move in on Christians, starting with something that is attractive and good. Then along comes the simplest argument, and division is already starting to take hold. We may walk away from it, "Well, I spoke truth." We can rationalize and justify our actions until we're blue in the face, but the bottom line is that this so-called good thing brought forth division. This is bad fruit. Always watch the fruit that is produced in each situation; this is how we can see if Jesus is present. When we begin to see that the fruit is bad, we need to repair it quickly before the chasm gets wider and wider. One time the Lord told me that division is almost the number one tool of satan because he can slow us down with it. Satan may know that he can't totally stop Christians, but he knows he can delay God's work, even for a whole lifetime.

"Now the serpent is the most cunning of all the animals that the Lord God had made" (Gn 3:1). That's interesting. God created satan. We don't want to forget this. Satan

30

would like us to forget this and believe that God and he are equals. This is not even close to truth, but at the same time, we must remember that satan is powerful. As our Holy Father said, satan is a terrible reality here; there is a lot of mystery (New York City News, 1978). In many of her apparitions Our Lady talks about how powerful and strong satan is, but we have to keep the balance and remember we have a God who is stronger, much stronger, and satan is merely a creature. The angels were made by God. Satan is not God, as much as he would like us to think that he has the intellect, the power, and the wisdom of God, he does not. He is not God.

Then the serpent goes on, saying to the woman, "Did God *really* tell you not to eat from any of the trees in the garden?" (Gn 3:1) He really didn't know for certain what God had said to Eve, so he started fishing for information, asking, "Did God *really* tell you not to eat from any of the trees in the garden?" (Gn 3:1)

Now, remember that Adam and Eve walked in great intimacy with God everyday. They were full of light, and when people are in prayer, there's a whole area within them where satan cannot come. There's an area within us that is so intimate with the Father that even our Guardian Angels don't come. So there are areas within us that satan does not know anything about unless we choose to tell him. But Eve chose to tell him what he obviously wanted to know. She said, "We may eat of the fruit of the trees in the garden" (Gn 3:3). Then she gives him the information that he is seeking. "It is only about the fruit of the tree in the middle of the garden that God said, 'You shall not eat it or even touch it, lest you die' " (Gn 3:3). Now he's got the information that he needed to know. He knows exactly what God said to her.

It is so important to know Truth, to know Jesus, because He is the same yesterday, today, and forever (Heb 13:8). He never changes. His truth always remains the

31

same. Whenever He speaks, whether it's His Word in Scripture, through His Church, or His word to us in prayer, He isn't going to change it or contradict Himself. He is the same. We can count on Him. We can believe Him. He is Truth.

Going back to the garden scene with Eve and the serpent, satan comes along and challenges God's word to Eve. He says, "You certainly will not die!" (Gn 3:4). He goes one step further, and then he's got her. He says, "No, God knows well that the moment you eat of it you will be like gods who know what is good and what is bad" (Gn 3:5). He knew her weakness. Satan fell because of his pride when he told God, "I will not serve." Misery loves company, and he's busy gathering his friends. Eve fell because of pride: it was her weak spot. It's incredible, but Eve believed the serpent as we ourselves sometimes do. Why? "The woman saw that the tree was good for food, pleasing to the eyes, and desirable for gaining wisdom" (Gn 3:6). This is the power she wanted. He went right to her weak spot—she wanted to know what God knew. See how clever this is? We especially need light at these times.

The irony of this is that the ability to know right from wrong is exactly what the Father wanted Eve to know, too. He wants us to know His mind and His heart. Everything He has, He has given to us through, with, and in Jesus. We don't become God or gods, rather we are always children of God, and He wants to draw us closer to Him. We are in God's family. In a family, parents always want their children to learn all they know, but as they draw closer together in relationship, the children don't become the parents of the family. They are not equal within the family in that sense. A child will always be a child within that family group. This is the close, intimate relationship the Father desires to have with us. He wants us to be His children. He will be the Father.

My father died at a very old age, but he was never anything to his little child but a parent. I was always his little girl. Age has nothing to do with the relationship. This is similar to our relationship with God. He wants us to know His mind and heart, but He is the Father, and we are not. He is the Holy One. We are not. But because He wants to share His light, His knowledge, and His understanding, they are always available to us. We already have these gifts. He gives these gifts to us through His Spirit. The Spirit is constantly trying to teach us how to use them.

St. Paul says, "The Spirit scrutinizes all matters, even the deep things of God" (1 Cor 2:10). Only the Spirit does that, so we go to the Holy Spirit whenever we need to know God's mind and heart in a particular situation. We ask Him, "What is Your mind and heart, O God? Will You share it with me?" Or like in Jeremiah 29:11, "I know well the plans I have in mind for you, says the Lord . . . A future full of hope."

We don't know God's plans, but He will tell us if He wants us to know. If He wants us to take the next step in His full light, He will tell us. "Father, what are Your plans? At least show me the next step of the plan." He usually doesn't show us the whole plan because He's loving, kind, and wise! We could stumble or become paralyzed in fear if we knew His total plan. We still have to grow spiritually! We wouldn't tell a five-year old something they will need to do when they are twenty. We don't give keys to the car to a little child until they are at least sixteen, and are quite certain they know how to drive. We have to grow into things, but we can ask for the next step in His plan to be illuminated for us.

After I came home from the cloister to begin this new ministry, God gave me so much direction, step by step about this call, that it was kind of overwhelming! It never bothered me in the convent not to know the next step because whatever I needed to know God would let me know. But now after I was home, I didn't know the next step, and I would run into the spirit of the world in very subtle ways through beautiful Christians. I would go to a prayer meeting every Saturday night full of peace and joy, and the people at the prayer meeting would say, "Do you have your community yet?" "No." "Well, when are you going to have your community?" "I don't know." "Well, do you have a place to live yet?" At this time I moved from pillar to post, wherever God provided, and I was happy. "No, I don't." "Well, don't you think you need a place? If you're going to have a community, you need a place to put people." "Well, yes." "Well, where is it going to be?" "I don't know." "Well, don't you think you should be doing something?"

I would come home every Saturday night from that prayer meeting so upset. These beautiful, beautiful people had no idea! They were just concerned. I was out here, alone. I didn't have a place to stay, no roof over my head, for any period of time. It would take me two or three days to return to peace again where I didn't have to know what God's plans were. I didn't have to know because the Father knew. Satan was robbing me of my peace, and soon I began to see the dynamic that was going on. Satan was using these beautiful people to get to me, and it worked, at least for three or four prayer meetings! But then God had mercy on me and let me put it together because there was a pattern developing. I began to see the repetition. That 20/20 hindsight is great, and I saw it. Now that I knew what was going on, I could go to the meeting and say, "No, no, but in God's good time, it'll happen when He's ready" and remain in God's peace.

But what also happened was that I would come home from the prayer meeting and ask, "Lord, what about this community? What about a place to live? And then when You do get the place and the community, how are we going to feed all these people? I know You can take care of me, but suppose I have another mouth to feed and another and another?" You know it can go on and on. Then the Lord told me, "Don't worry about those things. Those are steps two, three, four, and five." I asked, "Why can't I know about steps two, three, four, and five?" He said, "Because you would only get in My way!"

So don't become disheartened if you only know one step at a time because that's how He leads us, one little baby step at a time. He sees us as children and He loves us! When we are teaching a child to walk, it's just one little baby step at a time. The parent kind of moves backward, then the child moves forward, then the parent moves back a little bit more, and the child moves forward. The parents are always encouraging their child to take another step, a step that the child would never take if the parents had started out on the other side of the room. Well, God is like this, too! We truly are God's children. We are going to grow. We don't have to worry about that. We might think, "Oh my goodness. This is just one little step. I'm never going to get anywhere." But God is always moving, too, encouraging us to go forward, toward Him!

So Adam and Eve lost all that light. Then they saw themselves in the natural and saw that they were naked. They did not realize they were living so much in the Spirit, in the supernatural, and in such close intimacy with God until they lost these gifts. We lost all of them, too, except one: the freedom to choose. This is the one gift God let remain. The other gifts that were lost in the Fall are always in the process of being repaired within us, helping us grow stronger as we go more and more through the purification process.

Satan can strike at Christians through good things. As a new convert, I was on fire with zeal for the love of the Lord. I was madly in love with God and couldn't do enough for Him. I had a confessor and spiritual director who gave me a lot of freedom to develop my spirituality. Converts need direction because we tend to go to the extreme, and he watched me very closely. Every time I read anything about the saints, I wanted to do everything they did. I didn't realize at the time that each saint is individual, and we only are to do what God wants us to do. So I used to wish that I could read hearts like the Cure of Ars. So I'd eat boiled potatoes everyday because that's what he did. Or I'd wear a hair shirt because that's what some of the Carmelite saints did. Anytime I read about the saints, this is what I'd do. I wanted to become a saint, too. When I read about their severe fasting and penance, I thought, "If that's what it takes to become a saint, then I guess that's what I had better do." Nothing ever lasted very long. That's why my spiritual director let me do it, so I would get it out of my system! He knew it wouldn't last much longer than a week or two.

It was the beginning of Lent, and I was focused on fasting. Some very good friends of mine talked me into doing a fast on fruit juice during Lent. I thought, "Oh, it sounds wonderful to go into the desert and give up everything!" My spiritual director didn't really like this idea very much. He was hesitant, but finally said, "I'll tell you what we'll do. We'll try it and see how you are at the end of one week. Okay?" I said, "That's fine."

So I started and at the end of the third or fourth day, I began getting very tired. I had a full-time job and was very active in the Legion of Mary. I was extremely busy, and I was getting tired. My energy level was getting low, but I was bound and determined that I was going to make the full eight days of the fast. Now we see another dimension starting to take over that doesn't have anything to do with loving God or saving souls. It was sheer determination that I was going to do this so that I could get permission to do this for the rest of Lent. My motive was not good. I didn't have self-knowledge at that time. I couldn't see what was gong on. I didn't know my own heart. So at the end of the eighth day I looked awful and felt terrible. I had severe hunger pangs, my stomach hurt, and I thought, "Oh my. I wonder if this is what the saints went through."

My spiritual director saw this and said, "I don't think we should continue the fast, but if it would make you feel better, why don't you ask the Lord to show you how He looked at your fasting attempt. Ask Him to show you what He would like you to do." I thought, "That's very fair." So I asked the Lord to show me His mind and heart. I think this is when I had one of my first images. I don't remember having images before this. The image was of a beautiful, red apple, which now reminds me of the Garden episode, sin, but it didn't then. I saw this beautiful apple. It started turning slowly. It was like the Lord just wanted me to admire this apple. Then as He turned it all the way around, here was this ugly worm coming out of it! It just marred the whole thing. I thought, "What is that?" Then He said, and this was the first time He spoke to me about my fasting, "That's you. That's your self-love. In everything you are doing, you have self in it."

I was the head of Legion of Mary and doing all this wonderful, apostolic work, but it was always so that our Legion group could have more converts, more baptisms, more marriages fixed up, and more churches with perpetual adoration. Now that sounds wonderful, doesn't it? It sounds so zealous. Probably everyone else in our Legion group had the right motive, but it was as though I was driven, but not for the right motive. It was self mixed up with doing something for God.

This is the human spirit. Satan takes something good and can work in there to the point where it can cause our health to deteriorate. Then our apostolic endeavors will not bear the fruit. We will start to see after some time has passed that something is wrong—self! The human spirit is the most difficult spirit to discern because it's too close to us. We can't see our human spirit that well. We can see it in somebody else because we're objective, but we can't see it within ourselves. So we always need to check our discernment to see, "What spirit is moving if I pray this way? What spirit is moving if I take this action? Is it really the Holy Spirit? Am I moving in full concert with Him, or is this just me?" Satan is going to come in on any weaknesses, so I need to know myself, my weaknesses, and be able to discern my human spirit.

This summer a phone call came from someone who is being directed by one of our sisters at Bellwether. This young woman had walked into a Christian bookstore here and noticed there were not many children's books of the Holy Family and Jesus' childhood. When she walked into the bookstore and saw a book arrangement, the thought instantly came to her that the Lord wanted her to write children's books. She's a schoolteacher so she has a lot of experience with children. This would be a very natural thing for her to do. She thought it was the Lord, but she wasn't sure. Wisely, she called her spiritual director to check it out. She told her director, "Whatever you think, that's probably what I'm going to do. I think it's the Lord, but I need that confirmation from you." Now that's putting a lot on a spiritual director, so this sister who was the spiritual director called and asked me about it. I said, "I don't know. Let's take it to the Lord."

Don't ever be afraid to say, "I don't know." If we can't say that, then we're dealing with our own pride, too. We don't know. That's truth. That's the belt of truth. We may think we know, and if we're right, God will confirm that, too. But we don't know. We're always the little ones seeking the Teacher.

So when we sought God's mind on this situation, it was interesting that the Lord showed us this was her own spirit. She had always wanted to write a book. I asked her spiritual director, "Did she ever say anything to you that she'd always wanted to write a book?" She said, "Oh, yes. That's always been a deep dream of hers." Satan was using that. Then I thought, "Why would satan be so interested in her writing a children's book? It's a good thing. It would be a wonderful contribution to the Church." So when I put that before the Lord, "Why aren't You moving in this, and why isn't Your Holy Spirit inspiring her to write the book?" That's when the next step came, the deeper one. It was because God was calling her to a religious vocation. Deep down she knew it, and she was running from it. This would be a wonderful thing to do for the Lord, but this was not what He was asking of her. We never know. So she's not going to write the book!

Our own human spirit can be very deceptive. We do not know ourselves very well; we're too close. When we are too close, we can't be objective. Good discernment is to see which spirit is moving, to be objective. So it's easier to get discernment for other people because we're not part of it. We're not prejudiced or biased; we're in neutral. So when we're trying to get discernment in any way, we need to take time to get into neutral first. This can take a little while. It might take days. We might have to focus all our attention on begging for the grace to become neutral. St. Ignatius calls it "disinterested," where there's nothing in it for us. We're not part of it. If it happens this way, fine; if it happens that way, fine. We let God have the full authority to decide. It's still our choice to accept or refuse whatever God is asking or showing us. He's not going to touch the free will that He has given to us, but at least now in the discernment, He's going to show us His will, His preference, or the evil that could be lurking unseen. We may not discern properly on the first step or even the second, but He will continue to try to guide us in the right direction. He's going to turn on the light, fasten the belt around us, and show us the way.

So we always have to be careful. Satan comes disguised as an angel of light and brings us seemingly good things. For example, we may decide, "I'm going to make a resolution to pray an hour a day, particularly during Lent, Lord. That's the least I can do, giving You an hour every day." That sounds wonderful it if happens to be a Sunday and we're rested. Come Monday morning, it might be a struggle, but we know we made this promise, and we're going to keep it. Tuesday comes and it's getting a bit more difficult. Other things are on our mind. Wednesday comes and we may pray only thirty minutes. By the end of the week, we don't show up at all!

This can happen, and it's exactly what satan wanted. We can get grandiose ideas ourselves, thinking, "I'm going to do so much for the Lord." What may end up happening is that we do nothing, and discouragement sets in. "Lord, I can't even give You one hour a day." We start to think less of ourselves, and the next step usually is that we don't pray at all. Once discouragement comes, we usually stop whatever we are doing. Discouragement is probably the number two tool of satan. Discouragement is never of God. Satan uses it constantly to wear us down.

So we see a little of satan's strategy here, as well as in Genesis. Satan takes God's Word, and he changes it. He takes truth and distorts it ever so slightly. Satan's greatest inroad with Christians is probably that we don't take the time to check things out with God. Scripture says that Adam and Eve walked in intimacy with God every single day in this beautiful garden. Eve easily could have said, "I'd better ask God about this. I'll let you know if I'm going to eat it. Maybe I'll eat it tomorrow." But she didn't. So whenever we find ourselves too busy, hurried, or pressured because somebody is demanding a response right now, don't do it. Even if it's for a minute, ask, "Can I call you back?" Just disappear somewhere and check it out with God because satan likes those quick responses. He tries to fool us, "Don't ask God" because then we'll be in touch with truth and wisdom, and we'll know God's thoughts. Satan's attempts to trip us up will be exposed. We'll have the light and the knowledge. Satan is an agent of the dark, and if he can find ways and tactics to keep us in the dark, especially through busyness, that's what he'll use. There is the saying that satan will even sing in the choir loft if he can get us.

So **"Stand fast, with . . . the truth as the belt around your waist"** (Eph 6:14). The whole world is in the power of the evil one and that is what we're here for—to claim it back for the Lord!

Chapter 3

The Shield of Faith

*"In all circumstances, hold faith up
before you as your shield."*
Eph 6:16

So far we know that to stand fast we need the armor of
God, with the belt of truth, the Holy Spirit, around our
waist. Paul continues in Ephesians 6:16, "In all
circumstances, hold faith up before you as your shield."
The shield that Paul probably was talking about was a full-
length shield. It covered the entire soldier. Our shield,
faith, must cover us totally. Faith is our protection. What a
beautiful gift God has given to us! When we were
baptized, we were given three important gifts: faith, hope,
and love. As we're just coming into our new life, God
gives us this beautiful gift of protection, our faith.

Now as tiny babies we didn't know how to use these
gifts, but we did have faith in our parents. We believed that
when they picked us up, they weren't going to drop us.
When we were hungry, we believed that they would feed
us. We knew they would take care of us. This kept us
warm and protected. Faith keeps us protected. Faith is a
weapon, an extremely important part of our armor. As we
mature and start to use our gift of faith, it will begin to
grow.

This is true of all the gifts. If we use them, they will grow. We have the gifts of faith, hope, and love, but if we don't step out in love, initiate love, forgiveness, and all the other things that happen in love, then these gifts are going to become dormant and start to die. These gifts need to be used to be activated. We need to be constantly aware that we have these gifts, and then we must use them. Just when we think we have faith is usually when something happens that makes us realize that we don't have it at all! This stretching process is God's gift to us because it helps us to grow.

Look at dear little Peter. Everyone loves to use Peter as an illustration because he's so much like us! Look at how Peter loved Jesus. When Jesus called to him to get out of the boat, walk on the water, and come toward Him, Peter did. Now that takes faith. But Jesus wanted Peter's faith to grow, and I wouldn't be surprised if Jesus was kind of walking backwards to make Peter walk forward! All of a sudden, after using this faith to get out of the boat, Peter finds that he doesn't have the faith he thought he did. Peter must have thought, "Look what I'm doing! I must be crazy. I can't walk on the water!"

There is nothing natural about the gift of faith or any of these gifts. They are supernatural and are given to us to help us do supernatural things. I asked the Lord, "What kept You on the water? Peter didn't do very well." Jesus said, "My Father's love." Jesus was always held in the Father's love. The Father's love is what ultimately moves behind the gift of faith. It is the power of His love. The Father's love is like an engine in a car; it gives it the power to move. Once we begin to trust in that kind of love, then we begin to trust in the Person who is Love. We know then that this Love, the Father Himself, will carry us through.

We have to be careful of the saying, "Well, if we had faith we could walk on the waters. If we only had enough faith we could do this . . . ." There is a big difference

43

between presumption and obedience. To walk on the waters without being called upon those waters by the Lord and to think, "Well, here I am. God will hold me up" is presumption. This is presumption, and we're into sin. God may hold us up, and He may not! On the other hand, to walk on the waters because we have heard the Lord asking us to do so is faith. Trusting in someone else's strength, beauty, and goodness other than our own is faith. Faith is manifested through obedience. As I reflect on my own life, faith and obedience have never been separated. Faith and obedience really go together.

Satan will strike if we're not protected with faith. If we ever want to know if we are protected by faith, check to see under whose authority we are moving: our own, the Church's, our confessor's, our spiritual director's, or somebody else's. This is our safeguard. If we are moving under our own authority, we must be very, very careful. We may not be moving in a faith realm at all. Faith has to do with obeying what God is asking of us. Many times we may think, "I don't have enough faith to do that, Lord." This is humility because it is truth. It's okay to be at this spot where we're faltering, but then we ask for more. "Increase our faith, Lord. Lord, we believe, but help our unbelief." This is the prayer all of us can say every day. It isn't that we don't believe. We do believe, but He's always challenging us to move beyond our comfort level to a deeper level of belief, a deeper level of faith. God does this by putting certain circumstances in our lives that will help us grow.

One of the biggest situations that challenged my faith to grow was when God was calling me out of the cloister. It was a very terrifying experience for me in the early stages, and so it took very much discernment. After a year of numerous retreats, I finally made a thirty-day discernment retreat with a Devil's Advocate Board, which included a bishop. At this point it was finally discerned that it was the

Lord calling me out, not my own spirit or the enemy. This is what everyone was concerned about because satan would have loved for me to walk away from the cloister if it had not been God's will.

So now my leaving the cloister had been discerned, with many confirmations, even confirmations from spiritual directors, the retreat director, and the Devil's Advocate Board. Everything was in place. Everybody that needed to know that I was being called out knew. It was very clear what God was saying so I had the knowledge. I *knew*. I wasn't in the dark. The belt of truth was firmly in place. I had the knowledge and a lot of the specifics, but on the next to the last day of the thirty-day discernment retreat, the Lord indicated strongly to me, "No, not now. Yes, you have an authentic call. Yes, I'm calling you out but not now!"

This is important. We need more than just the knowledge of God's will, how it's going to happen, or when it's going to happen. Knowledge itself is not enough. We have to be careful. We may not understand His whole mind on a particular situation yet. Many times satan will try to get us to move on that insight right away before the whole knowledge has been given an opportunity to come into full bloom. We have power once we understand God's mind. So it surprised me when He was saying, "Not now." It was embarrassing because after this long ordeal I was going to have to tell all these people, including my own superiors, "I'm not going."

God directed me to St. Thomas Aquinas. I had never had a devotion to Thomas Aquinas, but I prayed to him for wisdom. In prayer Thomas said to me, "You do not have the authority of your own congregation. You have a vow of obedience to your congregation, not to any of these other people. Your congregation has not released you." There it was—that obedience! Once in the novitiate, I asked the Lord, "How does one know when one is really in authentic

45

prayer?" Now I was in the cloister and prayer is what we did all the time, so I asked, "How do I know if I'm really in authentic prayer?" My answer would have been, "It must be how much I'm loving. It must have something to do with love. When I'm loving, my prayer will bear fruit." But when I started reading Thomas Aquinas I learned, "The essence of prayer is obedience." This surprised me until I began to pray and think about it. The greatest manifestation of our love for God is obedience. Jesus said, "If you love Me, obey the commands I give you" (Jn 14:15). Obedience is the essence of authentic prayer.

We come to this authority situation again. This is what Satan seeks to constantly undermine within us as individuals, in our world, in our government, in our nation, and in the Church. He seeks to undermine the true authority of God and the way it is channeled through to us. Authority is key. So if we think we are people of faith, and hopefully all of us are, we must always ask ourselves, "Am I moving under God's authority? By whose authority am I moving?"

So I told them in the cloister, "I'm not going." They replied, "Well, everything is all arranged." I said, "Well, I just can't go. The Lord said, 'No, not now.' " "Oh, well, then when did He say?" I said, "He didn't say. He just said, 'Not now.' " So they sent me to another cloister. They were afraid that if I went back to my original cloister where many sisters knew I was being called out that when I actually did leave I might be splitting the community and taking some of them with me. I could understand this so I was sent to another cloister out West. It was wonderful! There were beautiful nuns and a beautiful superior. Nobody knew why I was there. They just thought I was another sister transferred in. I didn't mention this call again. I didn't mention it to anybody there, and I didn't mention it to the Lord. I could have said, "All this discernment! A whole year of this! If You have anything further to say to me, You can say it." But rather I thought, "Unless I'm ordered out of here by the proper authority, I'm not going."

Seven months went by. It was never discussed or brought up in my prayer. One day it was announced to the community that the Assistant General of the entire congregation was coming from Rome on a visitation. It was put this way; it was just a general visitation. She came, and when it was my turn to see her, she said, "Well, how is everything going?" I said, "Oh, just wonderfully." "Do you like it here?" "Oh, I love it here. I love the nuns. I love the superior." "Are you happy here?" "Yes." "Well," she said, "the reason I've come is to tell you that we've been watching you. We've been discerning your call also, and we feel it is God calling you out. We'd like you to go with our blessing." I'll tell you it was like the whole heavens came right into that room, and the Lord was smiling! He said, "Well, you asked for it. Here it is!" So on the Feast of the Transfiguration, I left the mountaintop and came home!

The reason I mention this story is because when we hear from God we have a tendency to think that whatever He is saying to us is going to happen now because God lives in the now. We may get a concept, prophetic word, or vision, and we think it's going to happen sometime on our agenda. When I came home from the cloister and things didn't happen the way I thought they were going to happen, I was concerned. The community didn't form immediately, and the property didn't show up when I thought it would. There were many things that didn't happen the way I thought they would happen. God had a different agenda. He still had a lot to show and teach me, and He still does.

This is the important point: had I not moved under this authority, satan would have used that day after day, gnawing away at me through doubt, undermining my faith. He would have used these doubts to get through my shield of protection until I started to go downhill. I can almost tell you what he would have been saying, "What are you doing out here? Who really called you out? By whose authority?" He would have used the same words that Jesus uses, but he would have twisted them. Satan used these same accusing words to Jesus as He taught in the Temple, "By what authority are you doing these things?" (Mt 21:23) He will accuse you, and it can get you off track and all turned around. I am so grateful to God for putting the brakes on that whole discernment retreat, even if it was just twenty-four hours before I would have gone, because it saved me so much harassment from the enemy. So the shield of faith is incredibly important, but it has to be manifested under authority. We can say, "I believe, I believe, I believe," but our saying these words doesn't hold any weight with satan. Only the fact that we believe in God and move under His authority holds any weight with satan. "I believe in God. I believe God is the One who asked me to do this or who said this. God is the One who is true here, not myself." Otherwise, satan will try to undermine our faith, and we won't be protected.

We have to really know ourselves. We may think, "Nothing could ever happen that would make me think Jesus is not present in the Blessed Sacrament because I have received that faith. I believe. I know. I know that I know that I know that He's there." If we get too sure of ourselves in any one area, what happens is that satan begins moving in another area? He loves to get us so focused in one area that we can even get proud of our gift of faith. He'll start moving in another area to take us off guard. He's sneaky, he undermines, he works in the dark, and he knows how to ambush and surprise attack.

We may feel strongly rooted in the teachings of the Catholic Church, thinking that nothing is going to undermine our faith. Then all of a sudden, we may start hearing this insidious little voice saying, "Who are you?

Do you really think that God loves you? Look at your sin. Look at your imperfection. Look at that." Then we start looking at some of these things, and we start questioning ourselves, "Do I really believe that God loves me?" This is where the big attack comes; the attack is not out there so much, but it gets very, very personal and hits us in our weak spots. Satan desires to undermine our personal relationships with the Father, Jesus, and Holy Spirit. He will undermine our relationship with Our Lady. "Do you really believe that God needs you, that He thinks that you're special? Do you really think you're a child of God's? Well, if you are, why don't you ever hear from Him?" Even in prayer the doubts can come. The attack comes all the time, and all we can do is be on guard and counterattack. So he'll start, "Why don't you stand on your own two feet? Why are you so co-dependent?" See how the spirit of the world speaks to us? Satan is behind the spirit of the world, and we have to be careful that we don't buy into whatever he's trying to hound us about because it will only undermine our faith in so many ways and cause immense destruction. We can respond to ourselves within our heart, "Why not? Why not be co-dependent and lean on God? Even more than lean, why not let Him carry me?"

Many priests come to Bellwether for private retreats. They come to rest, to come apart and be with the Lord, and they come for healing in different areas. One priest who came had already had a lot of prayer ministry from top people renowned in the healing gifts. Still he had two mental breakdowns, ten years apart, and had been totally removed as a pastor. When he came to our Center, at first I thought, "Lord, I wonder what it is you want to do for him here? He's had the best of ministry from the best people all over the world. So just show us as we go along what it is You want us to do, and why this constant depression won't lift."

This situation had an element of deliverance ministry involved, which is probably one of the reasons why he had come. When something is this prolonged, usually there are evil spirits behind it. We put him in retreat, assigned him Scriptures, and asked him to journal what was happening. Each day he showed up without his journal, and after three or four days, I began to see the deeper dynamic that was going on. When I started praying with him, I could see what the Lord was saying. This priest absolutely never prayed to the Father. So I backed up and found out that he was very, very abused by his father as a child, and there were a lot of hurtful memories.

But he had already had the best of inner healing. He had been through all that, and I thought, "Lord, that's not it. The depression isn't lifting. He still can't communicate with the Father." I thought, "Maybe there's unforgiveness here." Unforgiveness is a terrible block, probably the greatest block to communication. Now we were getting closer to what the problem is because he was having a difficult time accepting the fact that God is good, kind, and merciful. He couldn't feel this because God had allowed all these horrible things to happen to him. His concept of fatherhood was tremendously distorted and marred. But as we got deeper into it, I really did not see that there was unforgiveness. I think he had grown and had had so much ministry that he'd taken that step and had forgiven already. It was "the eleventh hour." All the Intercessors were praying their hearts out, "Lord, do something." Then the answer came. It was so simple: He couldn't believe that God loved *him*.

The reason I tell this story is because it has to do with doubt. He couldn't believe that God loved him. He had no love for the Father, so he had no real lifeline coming in. He lived in darkness, in his own world. The thing that kept him afloat was Our Lady. He could go to her. He had a good relationship with his own mother so he always went to Mary. He could believe in Our Lady's love for him, but he could not believe that the Father loved him. In fact when he did journal, he would get Scriptures like, "I have loved you with an everlasting love" (Jer 31:3) or "You are my beloved Son; on you my favor rests" (Lk 3:22), but he couldn't accept it. He couldn't believe. It cost him severe depression for at least twenty years and two mental breakdowns.

So once we saw what satan was doing, we took authority over the spirit of disbelief. We started praying for a new baptism and for the full gift of faith to be restored, and it was! It was wonderful. He had a tremendous breakthrough and has become a child now. He has come home to his Papa, his Abba. It is going to be a process for him to grow in this love, it'll take time to heal, but the lines of communication are open now.

Communication is extremely important because it is one of the tools satan uses to divide us. When people mis-communicate or don't communicate with each other or the Lord, they are opening themselves up to satan's attack through division. I don't mean communication when we're doing all the talking. Communication is when we are hearing and are connecting with God. It's a two-way dialogue. It's not a monologue; it's a dialogue. We have connected. Communication is extremely important. If we don't communicate with the Lord, we're going to be communicating with our own little inner voice or with satan. When Eve did not go back and communicate with God about what had been going on between her and the serpent, this is where sin entered. She didn't go and tell God. So the prince of the air, the ruler of darkness, was right there, eager to work powerfully in this communication.

When we read the statistics on divorce, the number one reason for divorce is lack of communication. Spouses don't speak to each other; there isn't any dialogue. This is division coming in through lack of communication. Division is satan's hallmark. This is one of the ways we can know he's been around. So I asked the Lord, "Why does satan work so much through communication?" One of the reasons He gave me was because the Second Person of the Trinity is the Word. Jesus is the Word of God. Obviously satan, who is Lucifer, must have been okay in serving the Word as the Second Person of the Trinity. The problem seemed to enter in when the Word, Jesus, decided, along with the Father and the Spirit, to become flesh, to become human. Once Jesus agreed to become one of us, this is when satan said, "I will not serve You in that form. I will not lower myself to do that. I will not." Jesus, the Word, who has become enfleshed in all of us, is where satan targets. This is why he loves to destroy us through communication. This is his way to get back at the Word, Jesus.

What is one of the ministries of Jesus as the Word? It's communication. This is what He does best. He communicates constantly between the Father and us. He is our link. This is intercession! Jesus is bridging the gap between His Father and us, so satan is constantly attacking the Word through words, through communication. Jesus chooses to communicate through us. So satan will attack us, and we must be careful how we use or don't use communication.

Dialogue is so important. Sometimes in misunderstandings the tendency is to withdraw. Sometimes silence is the most perfect thing to do. Sometimes to remain silent can be the most kind, the most loving, and the most charitable thing to do. But silence isn't always golden. Sometimes it's cruel, and gives the enemy an inroad because silence can divide. The longer the silence goes on, the more difficult it is to repair the hurt. So we have to be careful. Satan works powerfully through miscommunication or no communication.

We remember Eve not going back to talk things over with God, and this was the cause of her downfall. The same is true of us. If we are not communicating with God, we have an emptiness, a vacuum within us, and we have to be careful who is filling that space. If it's not God, then with whom are we communicating? Even if it's ourselves, then we need to move under someone else's counsel as well. We talk it over with someone we trust and wait for confirmation of whether or not this is the Lord. Hopefully our human spirit is moving with the Lord.

Sometimes I don't think we realize how close our spirits are with the Holy Spirit. We have to remember that it's not God way up there and us way down here, with satan all around trying to disturb us all the time. We have to constantly keep the balance and keep our focus on God who lives within us. He's very close. But again, these are things we believe, aren't they? Do you really, really believe all that Jesus has said to you? I thought I did. I started going through the New Testament to see what I believed of what Jesus said. I was looking for the things I really believed, things I lived morning, noon and night, sunny or cloudy, in season or out of season. I found a Scripture verse that was hard for me to believe, "Apart from Me, you can do nothing" (Jn 15:5). It has taken me about fifteen years to really believe this. It's not always easy to accept or believe the words of Jesus. We're intelligent people and there are a lot of things I can do. He said, *Nothing* without Me." He doesn't want to be left out of anything.

Think about the words, "I am with you always" (Mt 28:20). I didn't always believe that. I used to cry out, "Lord, where are you? Why have you left me? Help!" Yet Jesus says, "I am with you always." These are teachings of our faith. We can grow up hearing these words and yet never fully embrace them. These are the teachings of Jesus, and Satan will always try to undermine them, so we need to be firmly rooted in the teachings of Jesus.

When God speaks to us, we usually have a tendency to believe that it is God *at the time*. It isn't until maybe two weeks or two months down the line that the attack comes. "Do you really believe He said that? After all, you were on retreat and on a high then. That wasn't the real world. Now you have to deal with this and this . . . ." Satan can take something we firmly believe, distort it, and start to change it. This is what he did with Eve. He kept going back to Scripture and distorting it, changing God's words. This is satan at his best. We have to know his tactics and his strategies.

I was once directing a woman who truly believed she was being called to be a religious. I told her, "I think you need to make a retreat to get stronger in your call to religious life. You really need to hear from the Lord." Vocations don't come from what other people think we should do. We need to be called. We need to hear directly and deeply from the Lord, or we won't be steadied as the days and years go by.

So she did go on a retreat, and God was very gracious and spoke to her very clearly. She was in tremendous peace, and the decision was made to join the religious life. She went home, and a week hadn't even passed when she called and asked if she could see me. She said, "I've been thinking, and it's become very clear to me that it would be better if I married and became a successful wife than to become a nun and maybe be unfaithful." Look at how clever that is! This possibility of unfaithfulness had nothing to do with her call. God is looking for obedience, for people who will move under His authority. He'll heal us. He'll forgive us. He'll change us. He wasn't calling her to marriage. God was calling her to become a nun. Right away satan had started talking to her. You can almost hear his voice, can't you? "Why become a nun? You're going to be unfaithful and God isn't going to forgive you." That sounds terrible! She started to believe it and was ready to compromise her call. She was thinking she would become a wife and be successful that way. It wouldn't be as bad as being an unfaithful nun.

So even after we have believed God's word to us, satan can distort the message and our belief in it. We can't become complacent in our belief. Our belief that "God loves *me*" is one of the major areas and beliefs that satan will attack. We have to be careful of becoming complacent about God's love for us personally. This is what satan is ultimately trying to undermine all the time because this causes division and that's what he's after.

Moving only under Jesus' authority is so important in the faith realm. I can't begin to tell you how important it is. Everything about satan is disobedience. Yet everything about a Christian is obedience. The best way to come against this disobedience is through our obedience. One time I was in Medjugorje and could hear the little bells tinkling on the goats and sheep. I was praying, and the Scripture of Jesus separating the goats from the sheep came to mind (see Mt 25:32-33). I asked the Lord, "Why did you pick those two animals? Why sheep and why goats? For the goats to be totally separated from You for eternity, how awful." Jesus answered, "Watch them. Just take a look." So I did. As I watched, I soon saw that sheep are followers but goats are not. Goats don't need a leader; they're independent. God wants us to follow Him.

We need to constantly check out whose authority we are moving under. Are we being led at all times by the Holy Spirit, the Spirit of Jesus, and the Spirit of the Father? Mary and Joseph were led to Bethlehem. The Holy Family was led to Egypt. Jesus, as the Word, was led out of Nazareth and into the desert. Jesus was led to Calvary. Jesus was always being led, always moving under His Father's authority, not His own. This is extremely important for those of us who pray. We have to be discerning when we go into the desert, into the solitude to be alone with God because satan will be there, too. Satan moved into the desert when Jesus was there. Satan tempted Jesus in the desert, but Scripture tells us a little further on, "He left Him, to await another opportunity" (Lk 4:13). We're always going to be subject to the attack, to the temptation, but this is very much part of God's plan. When we're in the midst of temptation and trial, we grow. We get stronger, our faith grows, and God will be able to better use us!

The struggle itself isn't sin. It won't hurt us. If we open a cocoon ahead of its time, we will kill the butterfly because it won't have the strength to fly once it comes out. We have to let people go through the struggle. We have to let people experience the suffering, for this is where they grow and are strengthened. God allows this because after the battle we are stronger. There are many levels of the battle, and we have to gain ground as we move on. So temptation itself isn't sin; it's our opportunity to grow. Now what we do with the temptation is another story. We always want to make sure that we're the little lambs, the little sheep that is following. We must be the obedient ones, always moving under the authority of God as it is revealed to us in our lives and through the people whom God has placed in authority over us.

We're seeing so much deception today, so many attempts to undermine our faith. For example, let's take New Age. It has so many faces and is manifesting itself in so many ways, particularly under the guise of good. What's frightening about New Age is that it is coming under the guise of prayer, contemplative prayer. So I thought I had better learn about New Age because so many people were beginning to ask us questions. We bought books and tapes, and as we started to delve into the books, we just couldn't understand them. So we put the tapes on and there was just as much confusion for us from the tapes. "Oh that's it: confusion. That's how you spot it." Finally I just closed all the books and put the tapes aside, and said, "Lord, would you just teach me? There's got to be a simpler explanation for all of this. What's the root of this?" Nothing came. Later that night as I was just dropping off to sleep, with New Age the furthest thing from my mind, all of a sudden there it was. Pure gift. He said, "First of all, there's nothing new about New Age." This is one of the deceptions. Then He put it into the context of sin and of the Garden. It's when one wants to be center stage. Satan is behind it. It's original sin manifested at its best. All the focus is on me, myself, and I. That's the trinity that ultimately takes over: me, myself and I. God is not part of it at all.

New Age is very deadly. It's disguised in music, in our liturgy, and in our prayer. It's even disguised today in centering prayer; centering prayer that at one time was taught by the saints. Teresa of Avila, the great Doctor of the Church, the great mystic, taught it very well. There's nothing wrong with centering prayer when God leads it. We don't move into one stage of prayer on our own. God leads us into these different stages of prayer. The way centering prayer is being taught today is that if we do this and this and this, and get all these distractions out, controlling it, then God will do what He is supposed to do. Man has totally taken over again. This is not centering prayer. This is another dynamic, and what it is doing is creating an emptiness and vacuum in people who may not yet know the Lord that well. So when different experiences happen they may not be able to discern who is speaking. Wherever there is emptiness or a vacuum that is not filled by God, satan will come and fill it himself.

Jesus said, "I know my sheep and my sheep know me. They know my voice" (see Jn 10:4,14). This is why in our prayer it is good to always stay close to Scripture and not just to go into this emptiness, hoping that something will happen. God will lead us into mysticism. We are all called

57

to be mystics. God wants it, but it comes by learning what is on His mind, the revelations of His heart, like the great contemplative John. It's all gift. Contemplation, true mysticism, is gift. It all comes from God. We do nothing but ask for it and then receive it.

Another dimension where we see the enemy working very powerfully today is in the homosexual, lesbian, and the transsexual dimension. The Lord taught this to me when I had only been out of the cloister a year. I was living in the caretaker's quarters at a doctor's house. Father DiOrio was coming into town, and some man had driven to Omaha from across the country, wanting some confirmation regarding transsexual surgery. Fr. DiOrio was unable to see him privately so we received a phone call asking if we would see this person. I never had heard of a transsexual before. I didn't know what the word meant, but I said, "Yes, we will pray with him. No problem." So that night, I went and told my doctor friend that this man was going to show up tomorrow. I asked him, "What's transsexual?" He said, "Where did you hear that word?" I said, "Well, he's coming tomorrow." "He is? I suppose you're going to be praying with him?" I said, "Yes." He said, "Well, I want you to have a priest there. You'd better have your prayer team, too. I don't think this is a good idea." I said, "Please tell me what this is." So he did.

I went over to Mass the next day and prayed, "Lord, I don't think I know what I'm doing. I don't think I know what You want me to do." So the Lord started to direct me, "Ask him about his childhood. You'll see why he wants to change his gender. The answer is here." So I found out that this person did not know his biological father. When he was about four years old, his mother remarried and had a child, a little girl. All he knew was that this little baby girl was in the family now and was getting all the attention from daddy, who was her biological father, but not his. The only reason he could figure out why this was happening was that she was a girl, and he was not. So right then he started putting on long dresses, playing house, and doing all the things that little girls do, trying to be like a little girl so that he could be loved by his daddy. As he grew up, he forgot all these thoughts but subconsciously there remained the thought, "This is how God made me."

I didn't know all this. All I was getting from the Lord was, "Ask him about his childhood. Then start praying. I'm going to lead you and show you what to do." The Lord said, "Let's go back and image for him the way I created him male." So this is what I did. I said, "We're going to go back in your imagination. I want you to image the way God created you." We brought in the image of the Trinity there. We had God start forming the different parts of the body, the head, and the face. We went through all of this as God was showing this to me. As we got to the genitals, his whole body started to shake. He got very upset, and I knew we were up against evil spirits. He said, "No, no. You're lying. That's not true. God created me to be female. He always wanted me to be female." So we just stopped the ministry, took authority over the spirits, and got rid of these spirits that had lied to him. In Scripture, it says, "Male and female He created them" (Gn 1:27).

So the Lord said, "Start again." So we started again, and this time when we got to imaging him male, no problem at all. In fact, the ministry ended with him knowing that God had always wanted him to be His little boy, and what a privilege it was to be created male because Jesus was created male. Now he could identify with Jesus, and he saw what an honor and a beautiful thing it was to be male. He ended up singing the "Our Father" for us. It was beautiful! Satan was using deception, this lie to deprive him of the fullness of life.

Deception is moving through our culture very powerfully today. Satan is trying to get us to think that this deception comes from every area other than from him. We think this deception comes because of our background or because we have inherited it. We are being tricked into believing that since people think I'm this way, I'll always be this way, nothing's ever going to change. This is deception, and it is coming from the enemy.

This past year a beautiful housewife showed up at our Center. She had several small children and had been very depressed for a long period of time. She had the best counseling but it didn't help. When she told me her story, the bottom line was that she had fallen in love with a woman and felt she was being called more into a relationship with this woman than with her husband. She believed that God really wanted her this way. This is deception. Deception always comes through our woundedness. When people are lonely, when they're not happy, when there is some emptiness that is not being filled or some need not being met, there's an opening that allows the attack entrance. She had a brother who was a priest, and she had already talked to him. She knew the teachings of the Church. So I asked the Lord, "Why do You have her here? We're not counselors or psychiatrists. Other people know the theology of the Church much better. Yet her faith and belief in who she is and who You created her to be has been distorted and undermined by satan. Show us what You want us to do."

I told her, "You've heard from your parents. You've heard from your husband. You've heard from priests. You've heard from psychiatrists. The one person you haven't heard from is God. Would you like to hear from God?" That's when I knew why she'd come. We both knew she needed to hear from God. I said, "Why don't you spend the weekend in one of our chapels here with the Blessed Sacrament. Just spend it with Jesus and listen. Listen to whatever He's going to say or show you."

So we got the Intercessors praying! We took authority over the spirit of doubt that had totally undermined her faith. We took authority over other spirits as God was showing them to us. We can do all that in intercession; a person doesn't even have to be present or know we're praying for them for our prayers to be effective. We hardly ever cast out spirits in the presence of the person in order to preserve their dignity and not frighten them. The spirits can hear you wherever they are. They can be anywhere in the world, and the spirits will know when we are speaking to them. So we took authority over these spirits, got them inactive, and asked God to do the rest.

She arrived on a Friday night, and on Sunday morning she came to me, tears just streaming down her cheeks and said, "I've never been so loved in all of my life as I've been with the Lord here." She started sharing some of the things that God was letting her understand about herself. He was showing her how beautiful she is and how He made her the way He'd made her. He showed her her relationship with Himself as a man, Jesus as a male, and He showed her her relationship with her husband. It was beautiful. She was healed that quickly!

Healing lesbianism isn't easy because women are such heart people; they get into heart-to-heart relationships. Homosexuality doesn't have quite the same depth. So there are very few healings in lesbianism. The power here was in the deliverance: in the binding and casting out through the power of God's love. It goes together; the binding and then reinstating them with the belief, "I am good. I am lovable. I am loved by God." No human love can fill this space that belongs to God. There's a part in all of us that's reserved only for God.

We know that even when there is ninety-nine percent truth, it's not God. This is what we're always looking for in prophecies and messages from visionaries and inner locutionists all over the world. We're always discerning. At first glance some of these messages may look very good and true, but we must always be looking for that one or two per cent that isn't true. Satan can speak truth. I did not know this at one time. He can quote Scripture accurately so we can't let this be our guide. We have to know who is quoting Scripture to us. Satan quoted perfect Scripture to Jesus in the desert, but Jesus came back with "Scripture also has it..." (Mt 4:7). Jesus knew who was using Scripture. Satan will use Scripture, the Word of God, and he will speak truth.

One of his titles from the Book of Revelation is "the accuser." He will speak through other people and accuse us. Be careful of this. Don't even get into a dialogue with accusation. Just take it to the Lord. The way the Lord taught this to me was when I was still in the cloister. I was getting ready to come home. I was just waking up, and I heard this whole conversation going on like in a canyon where I could hear an echo. I thought, "There's nobody there." Then as this voice got louder and stronger, I realized it was satan standing in the presence of the Father, accusing me of all of my sins, of everything I've ever done wrong. I'm telling you, he didn't miss one! I couldn't believe it! It seemed like a litany that went on and on and on. When he was finished, you could hear a pin drop.

Then the Father spoke to me, "Do you have anything to say?" Well, I knew that everything satan said was true. I knew it, and I'll tell you, when you're in the presence of the Father, you're in pure Truth. That's light. So, I answered, "Guilty." Instantly I saw the image of Jesus standing right there. I hadn't even noticed He was standing there right beside me. He had on a deep, long, red mantle, which was His Blood. He was totally covered in the Blood of the Lamb, and He took one arm with this mantle and clothed me with it and said to the Father, "Not guilty!" So the Blood of the Lamb will come against satan even if he's telling the truth. We stand on faith that Jesus has redeemed us by the Blood of the Lamb. Jesus loves me!

Therefore, **"In all circumstances, hold faith up before you as your shield"** (Eph 6:16). My faith and belief in Jesus' love for me will keep my shield in place. It will keep my eyes focused on Jesus and keep me protected from all harm. When I was a little girl in Sunday School, we would sing a song, "Jesus loves me this I know for the Bible tells me so. Little ones to Him belong, they are weak but He is strong!" Amen.

Chapter 4

The Helmet of Salvation

"Take the helmet of salvation ...."
Eph 6:17

St. Paul says, "Take the helmet of salvation." This is the mind of Jesus Christ. Wouldn't it be wonderful to have the mind of Jesus? To think like Jesus, to know what He knows, and to reason like Jesus may sound simple. Imagine living in the constant presence of the Father! Imagine what it would be like to interact with other people as Jesus did. He could interact perfectly with enemies or friends, sick people or well people, strangers, and possessed people. But for us it's not this simple. This is the great battlefield of our minds. We look for the enemy everywhere but where he lurks—right here in our minds.

The mind is where he got to Eve, and this is where he will get to us, too. Most often we can't control our first thought. A stray thought can happen, even from outside of ourselves, but what we do with that thought is our choice. How we entertain it, how we move with it or against it, and how we let it take us up or take us down is our choice. This is the constant discernment process that is based on knowing ourselves and being aware of the choices that we are going to make.

The enemy works through the mind in many different ways. One of the most effective and common ways he affects our mind is through negativity. I don't know what it is that makes a negative thought easier than a positive thought, except that it's easier to go downhill than to go uphill! Maybe there's a spiritual law of gravity, too! So here comes the first thought, and it's negative. Whatever our response is will determine where we're going. If our response is negative, we're probably on our way down, and if we don't catch it on the second or third thought, the negativity will gain tremendous momentum. We'll be cascading into all kinds of other thoughts that will bring us down quickly.

Has that ever happened to you? We can wake up in the morning and really feel wonderful. Then something is said or a thought comes. We may toy with it, dialogue with it as Eve did, and before we know it a lot of memories start coming. Other dialogues that didn't get handled are starting to surface, and before we know it we're down in a deep, dark pit. We're in darkness. We're in enemy territory. It all happens in the mind. If we can remember that we want to stop the process, and on the second thought take it uphill, take it to the Lord, take it to the Holy Spirit, we'll be in good shape. We'll receive a strength and a power, a light and a truth, and knowledge from the Lord to keep us protected in His kingdom. The gifts of the Holy Spirit of wisdom and discernment will become more activated, and the negative thought will lose all power to drag us down.

Those in the early Church made their choices, decisions, and discernments a little bit differently than we do today. Scripture says, "It is the decision of the Holy Spirit, and ours too" (Acts 15:28). The way we often make decisions today is that we will talk about the pros and cons of something, and then we'll make the decision. Then we'll take it to the Lord to see if our decision was okay. If we can learn to walk with more of an awareness of the indwelling God, with the Spirit of the Lord, as those in the early Church did, we would be much better off. It's much easier if we go to the Holy Spirit right away and ask Him to come and give us counsel. Before we get involved in anything, we need to invite the Holy Spirit into whatever is going on. We need to invite Him to come into our initial thoughts, into whatever is going on in our minds, bringing it to Him right away because He Himself is the answer. The Lord will bless us as we bring our needs and concerns to Him first.

The Holy Spirit will direct us, and then we will know what to do. We may find out that some things are not of the Lord right away, and so we will stop the process. There may be some thoughts that the Lord wants us to entertain and respond to, which may even involve confronting or defending a truth. There's nothing wrong with that, but don't enter into it alone. We follow the lead of the Holy Spirit. He will always be there with us. Jesus said, "Apart from me, you can do nothing" (Jn 15:5). So we must learn to go to the Lord for everything, and we'll be safe. This is having the mind of Jesus, the helmet of salvation.

Jesus was so totally and utterly dependent upon the Father and the Spirit of the Father dwelling within Himself that He said, "The Son cannot do anything on his own but only what he sees the Father doing" (Jn 5:19). Jesus was a grown man, thirty-two or thirty-three years old, and even as He was getting close to death He continued in obedience. He consulted the Father at all times. He walked in the perfect will of always pleasing the Father. So don't be ashamed to be dependent upon the Lord; don't be ashamed to be vulnerable, to be little, to lean on God, and to be a child.

Did you ever wonder why Jesus often called His disciples, grown men, little children? I don't know what they must have thought. Probably nobody had ever called them little children before. They were pretty rough, tough, and weathered to be little children. We, too, are God's little children. If we keep our identity as God's children straight, we won't have any problem going to the Lord with everything.

I had a superior in the novitiate who used to tell me, "Your thoughts mold you." I really had little idea of what she was saying then, but those words have come back to me many times since. Our thoughts do mold us. She would also say, "I can't hear a word you're saying because your actions are shouting."

Our thoughts mold us, and we act very much out of what we think. There's nothing wrong with this if we are remaining as God's children. Children are so pure and transparent. They are spontaneous. Whatever they're thinking on the inside, it's right there on the outside. There's no falsehood. It's beautiful. This is how Jesus wants us to be. He wants us to be like little children so that whatever is going on inside us will truthfully have its full expression on the outside. Our words, our relationships, and our actions will show who we are. God wants there to be no duality or hypocrisy within us, and simplicity will be the fruit that flows from this.

The world we live in today makes fun of simple people. "Oh, it's so simple," as though there's something wrong with being simple. God is simple. It is very difficult to become simple. In arranging a room it's difficult to get simplicity, but when you've got it, it's beautiful. There is a beauty and an ease in simplicity whether in dress, speech, or lifestyle. Simplicity is difficult to attain because we are very complicated. Original sin has taken away our simplicity and made us very complicated. So we have to become more Godlike. God is simple. God is childlike. God is focused. A child is focused. A child can only see one thing at a time. You can only tell a child one thing at a time. You can't even tell a child when his birthday is.

They don't understand next week, next month, next year; that means nothing. They live totally in the present moment. So does God. There isn't any tomorrow with God. There is only today. So those of us who think we have tomorrow have bought part of the lie. We do not have tomorrow. Tomorrow has never been lived by anybody. This is the first time we've ever lived this day. What a gift God gives us each day: to live each day to the hilt and then to return it to Him with love.

Awareness of the present moment is so important to keep the mind pure and to keep the enemy out. The enemy always likes us to live outside the present moment. He likes us to live in the past, or he wants us to look ahead to the future. Have you ever noticed that? Subtle, isn't it? It's something we do almost automatically, always looking back or worrying and wondering about tomorrow. God lives only in the present moment. We need to become aware of this, too. If we live outside of this moment, we can miss all the graces and the beauty that God has for us right now. We call it the Sacrament of the Present Moment. It's beautiful. It's the Sacrament of the Present Moment because God is present now. He's here now. All the grace and beauty are present right here, right now, in His presence. It's so amazing that God, who is not confined by time, chooses to live here with us now every moment of every day in the present.

In Romans 12:2 we read, "Do not conform yourselves to this age, but be transformed by the renewal of your mind, so that you may judge what is God's will, what is good, pleasing and perfect." Good decisions are made this way. Through the renewal of our mind God always wants us to make the most perfect decision, not just what is better, but what is the very best, what is perfect.

We see this in the story of Mary and Martha. Both women loved Jesus, and Jesus loved them. He is in their home and was very comfortable there. Obviously He

68

visited them a lot. Dear Martha was doing a beautiful work serving Jesus. Those of us who have guests at our homes love to serve. This is why so many of us are in one kind of ministry or another. We love to serve God's people, we love to serve Jesus, but Jesus said that there was a better choice. He was giving Mary the "better portion." Dear Martha was serving Him food, but Jesus, in the meantime, was feeding Mary! "Mary has chosen the better portion and she shall not be deprived of it" (Lk 10:42).

There is a Martha and a Mary in each of us, whether we're a man or a woman. The Mary part resides in the will. This is where we make choices, and it is through these choices that we receive. This is the higher faculty of the soul where we receive. This is where the gift is given. The Martha part is where we do and serve. We need both the Mary and the Martha part. What a world this would be if there were just Marys. When I went into the cloister, I thought all the sisters would be Marys. Well, everybody is both. We worked hard in the cloister. There was a lot of work and a lot of prayer. So it's not either/or, it's and/both. We need to serve, but we need to be served by the Lord. He said, "The Son of Man has come, not to be served by others but to serve" (Mt 20:28). So we need to let Jesus serve us and meet our needs. We need to let Him constantly purify our minds and fill us with deeper hope, which basically is the helmet of salvation.

"We who live by day must be alert, putting on faith and love as a breastplate and the hope of salvation as the helmet" (1 Thes 5:8). Isn't that beautiful? Hope. What's the opposite of hope? How does the enemy work in our mind? If we don't have that helmet of salvation on, we can sink into fear, despair, discouragement, depression, and unforgiveness. We see this is all enemy territory, and it can lead to severe depression where we lose hope and start going down. We can even become suicidal. We have to be aware of our thought life constantly so we can fight. The real battleground, where the real fight is fought, is in our own minds. So we have to get hope back and keep it firmly in place. Our thoughts must be protected. We have to go to the Lord constantly for help. The battle is the Lord's, even when it is in our own minds.

Satan will always go after the person who is in warfare because if he can knock out the warrior, then look at all the ministry that's gone. Look at all the prayer that will be stopped. Satan can work and cause much destruction through our thoughts. When we get discouraged, depressed, and aren't dealing with our angers and emotions, what happens to our prayer? What happens to our relationship with God? It all goes downhill. When we're angry with someone, we may not have a confrontation. We might just stuff our feelings and sit on them, but then we will need to watch our actions. Usually we will start to avoid that person. "I'm not angry. I just don't want to be around you any more." Satan is busy at work causing division through our thoughts.

I used to stuff my anger. I was raised in a household where there didn't seem to be any anger. The only anger that I saw would be in movies where people would shout and scream at each other. If somebody got angry, there was a lot of expression. I didn't ever experience that personally, so I grew up thinking I'm not an angry person. Well, I just called it another name and didn't know it! All our emotions are gifts from God. He took me through all of the beautiful emotions that He has given to us, one by one. He showed me how we use them in our unredeemed selves and how we are to use them in our redeemed selves. He showed me that these gifts of our emotions have to be transformed through the constant renewal of our minds, changing our thoughts for His thoughts, changing our feelings for His feelings, and changing our emotions for His emotions. We have to use these gifts in a positive way rather than in a negative way.

The first time He taught me that we are to use these gifts in a positive way was with a priest I loved dearly, who had been my confessor and spiritual director for a long time. I noticed we weren't agreeing on everything, and up until this point, we had never disagreed on anything. Maybe the Lord was allowing this experience to teach me. I was having a hard time agreeing with him, so I was just responding with, "Uh huh, uh huh, hm." I didn't know how to handle it. So instead of making my feelings known, I was stuffing them, but I wasn't really agreeing. Finally he said something that was the last straw, and then he said, "You didn't answer me at all this time. Is something wrong? Are you angry?" Well, I thought, "My goodness, nobody gets angry at a priest." I said, "Uhm. No, no, Father, I'm not angry." "Oh, really? Well, how are you feeling right now?" I just blurted out, "I could just wring your neck!"

This is when I began to see I had another terminology for anger. I did have anger in my life; I just called it something else. The Lord reminded me of how I had gotten angry at my big brother when I was a teenager. I didn't know how to express my anger, so I went up to my bedroom and slammed the door with all my might. I felt wonderful! This is anger, and we all have different ways of expressing it.

Once we have self-knowledge, we will know and understand our emotions better through how we act and react. This will help keep the helmet of salvation firmly in place. When we are in a situation and find ourselves overreacting, we are acting out of something that's wounded within ourselves. We need to take a look at our overreaction with the Lord to get His perspective on this situation. We need to look at things with the Lord under His microscope. If we don't, satan will try to take over and get us to look at things through his eyes, stirring our emotions, and the situation will get magnified. It will grow like a cancer, and then we will really need help. So we have to be very careful here and only move forward after we know what God's thoughts are on this matter.

When asked, "How often must I forgive?", Jesus replied, "Seventy times seven" (Mt 18:22). His answer was a tremendous shock to Peter and the apostles because forgiveness was never required before then. Imagine what it would have been like to live in the Old Testament where we didn't have to forgive anybody? "An eye for an eye, a tooth for a tooth" (Mt 5:38). It may sound good to us sometimes, but Jesus comes along and says no, this is the New Testament now! "When a person strikes you on the right cheek, turn and offer him the other" (Mt 5:39). We are going to forgive. We are even going to forgive those who are our enemies. We are going to forgive those who persecute us and actively strike against us. We are going to forgive. It is as if Jesus said, "It'll be okay because I'm going to give you the power to do it. Forgiveness is a gift, and I'm going to give it to you now." He did. He breathed on them Easter night. He walked through those closed doors and breathed His Spirit, His risen Spirit, His Holy Spirit into them so that they could forgive (Jn 20:19-23). Now if Jesus can walk through locked doors, He can walk into locked hearts, can't He? He can breathe that forgiveness into any of us.

There's a person right here in Omaha who was married and had a young son in grade school. He was a paperboy, and he was murdered. It was an occult type murder where he was tortured severely for three days and carved with a knife. It was a terrible thing, something, which would be very difficult to forgive. It's very extreme, but forgiveness always begins with making a choice to forgive. The father of the boy made a decision, "I do want to forgive." But in humility, he could only say to the Lord, "I cannot forgive now but I want to, and I know that with Your grace, You will help me." That was the choice he was making, but his wife made another choice. Her choice was not to forgive; she chose the revenge, "an eye for an eye, a tooth for a tooth. This man who killed our son deserves to die." She became more and more bitter and resentful, and the marriage ended in divorce.

We can see how satan came in with his destruction, but it was not total destruction. The father, on the other hand, made the decision, "I want to forgive." He began seeking God's grace, and as time went on, his hurts began to heal. One day he was making the Stations of the Cross and on the Fourth Station Our Lady spoke to him. He had been begging God for this grace to forgive. He wanted to forgive but he knew he needed extra help in order to do this. I don't think he had ever heard Our Lady speak to him before or since then, but she called him by name and said, "You know, we have something in common." He said, "We do? What?" She said, "We both have a son who was murdered!" And he was healed! He could identify with Our Lady's pain. He saw how she had handled it.

If we can identify right away with the pain of Jesus or the pain of Mary, our healing is going to happen more quickly. United and strengthened by Mary's suffering, he was now able to begin the real forgiveness process. Today he witnesses to the healing power of forgiveness, particularly to divorced couples who have a very difficult time forgiving. He is being used as a powerful instrument of the Lord for these particular graces of forgiveness. So, wonderful fruit came forth for him from this terrible situation. Satan did not get a stronghold in his mind, and this situation has brought him closer to the Lord and to Our Lady.

There was a nurse who worked with children who came to see me. She was falling apart. She had been seeing psychiatrists for several years, but she was still going downhill and didn't know what to do. For some reason nobody was able to help her. The doctors would medicate her, but the problem was not being resolved, and she was getting worse. She was becoming a recluse and couldn't bear to even be around her little children anymore. She couldn't even drive anymore and was going to lose her job. The situation was getting quite serious. I had no idea of what to do to help her, which is really a blessing because that forces me to ask the Lord. He said, "Just let her talk. Wait a few sentences now. It's going to come, and you're going to hear it." I thought, "He could have told me," but He wanted me to listen at another level. So she was talking about her problems and her job situation, and all of a sudden, she said, "You know, a thought just came to my mind. I haven't thought of this in years, and it just occurred to me that I have never told this to anyone. I didn't even remember it." I said, "Really, what is it?" She said, "When I was nineteen years old, I was engaged to be married. It was several days before the ceremony. I went to the doctor for an examination, and the doctor raped me. It was such a horrifying experience that I broke off my engagement." The wedding was off, and somehow she shut down that part of her with all those feelings. Those feelings of hate would come and the pain with it, but then she would just block them off from her mind. The enemy had come in there, and twenty years later her life was practically in ruins.

I simply asked her, "Can you forgive the doctor?" She said, "No! Never. Never. Never." So I said, "Lord, help!" We're always talking to the Lord on the inside, "What should we do?" He told me, "Reset the scene. Take her back and I'll go with her." So I asked her permission to do this, "Could we reset the scene in the doctor's office, but let Jesus go there with you this time and see what happens?" She agreed. I told her, "You're going to have to let me know now where you are, what's going on, and we won't go any further until you let me know when Jesus shows up. So I waited, and pretty soon she said she was in this examination room, on the examination table. Then she said, "Oh, Jesus just came through the door." I thought, "Thank you, God. Thank you, God." In ministry, we are interceding all the time, "Lord, please show up." It's out of our control; the control is always the Lord's, and we never know what He's going to do. That's a blessing for us because then we stay out of His way!

So Jesus was in the examination room and I said, "Is the doctor there yet?" She said, "He's just coming into the room now." So I waited and then said, "Can you share what's happening now?" She said, "You'll just never believe this. When the doctor came into the room and saw Jesus there, the doctor burst into tears and began to sob uncontrollably. Jesus took the doctor into his arms and held him and comforted him. The doctor begged Jesus for forgiveness for what he had done and Jesus forgave him." I said, "What do you see now?" She said, "Oh, I see a broken man. I see a man who knew that what he had done was wrong and he is repenting. He is sorry." She said, "I have a feeling I'm not the only woman that's involved in this." "How do you feel toward the doctor now?" "I feel so sorry for him." I asked again, "Can you forgive him now?" "Oh, yes!" She was healed! She was healed of that poison.

When we don't forgive, either consciously or unconsciously, we block God's grace. It's like the stone that was in front of the tomb being rolled away and Jesus coming forth from the tomb. Unforgiveness is like the stone that keeps us locked in a tomb. When we refuse to forgive another, it keeps us in a death and dying situation. We are the ones who end up broken and hurt, not the person who is the one we need to forgive.

When we forgive someone else, God can continue to use us and our prayers as intercessors to help other people, particularly the person who hurt us. If we can't forgive this person, then our prayers for this person are blocked. We have blocked God's grace from being channeled through us. See how that works? The person that hurt us is often the very person we do not want to pray for. But when we do not pray for the person who hurt us, the healing that person needs may be withheld because we are not allowing God to use us as an instrument of his peace and of his healing and presence. Forgiveness is very important! It always goes two ways. Forgiveness opens us up so that our communication is kept directly with the Lord. Then we can be constantly filled with His love so that we can give that love away. One time the Lord told me that to withhold love from anyone is to withhold life because love is life.

There is so much death in the world today because so many people are not being loved. There are spirits who can live in our emotions. We call these spirits "ministering spirits" because they enter through our emotions and "minister" to us. They "help" our emotions along.

For example, we may be angry all the time and never repent of it. We may rationalize our feelings, thinking, "It's okay. I have a right to feel like this." Maybe we do and maybe we don't, but if these feelings of anger are not being confessed and brought into the light, they can build a house of anger within us. An evil spirit of anger can come and live within, and the anger will begin to control us. Then we lose control. All of a sudden, we may find ourselves awfully irritated about something. We may feel the momentum picking up. There is a power working that is helping our anger along. When we see this happening, we need to stop right away and say "Wait. The momentum is rising. I'm blowing this all out of proportion. What's going on?" When we find this happening, we need to go to the Lord and ask His opinion. If we don't come against our emotions, we may be allowing a spirit to take over to use us to hurt someone or magnify something out of proportion. We go into the unredeemed self, the self that forgets about God and His love, and focus only on poor little old me.

Ministering spirits live in our unredeemed self. They come and go in our thought lives and unhealed emotions. They begin in our thoughts. When we entertain these negative thoughts and emotions and don't take the steps necessary to heal these emotions or negative thoughts, these ministering spirits can enter our heart and live there. Because we have invited these ministering spirits in through our negative feelings and thoughts, they are much more difficult to remove because our will is involved.

Ministering spirits can come and enter if we open the door for them, especially through unhealed emotions. So if we don't have the helmet of salvation on, if we are not focusing on God's hope and presence in our lives, we can let them in, and they can influence our actions. These spirits can cause a lot of pain and suffering within us. They can delay God's work as they cause us to focus on ourselves and not on God. They can delay whatever God wants to do for others through us, especially in our own family situations.

This often happens in the area of the seven capital sins: covetousness, envy, gluttony, anger, lust, pride, and sloth. For a long time I didn't realize that these capital sins are actually high-powered spirits. They are tools and agents of satan. They're not just sins; they are controlling spirits. We may think of sin as a thing rather than realizing that there is someone behind these sins. This is where we have to be so careful not to allow the sun to go down on our anger or any hurtful emotion. We do not want to allow sin to find a home within us. If these emotions fester within us, these spirits can come and get very comfortable living within us. We can form habits, get very comfortable with these habits, and before we know it, we may be led by a spirit other than the Holy Spirit.

In Revelation we read, "Then another sign appeared in the sky: it was a huge dragon, flaming red, with seven heads and ten horns; on his head were seven diadems" (Rv

12:3). There is much speculation about what these seven heads could be, but one of the interpretations the Lord has taught us is that they are the seven capital sins. When the capital sins are not checked and are allowed to run rampant, they are powerful and destructive. We are seeing these capital sins on a large scale today, and they have a tremendous hold.

These capital sins are tools of the dragon and are manifesting themselves in our culture through all this busyness. Busy, busy, busy! It's amazing! Before our forefathers and our grandparents could put butter on the table, they had to milk the cow and churn the butter. They had to do every little thing themselves to put one meal on the table. Now with convenience foods and microwave ovens we can put a meal on the table in no time. We have all these time savers, but why isn't it freeing us up for more time? We have less time today than they did before. We hardly have time to smell the flowers. People come to me wanting me to be their spiritual director, but there's nothing to direct because there's nothing spiritual going on. There's no time to pray. Guess who's moving through our busyness?

This rush is in every aspect of our lives, and it's robbing us of life. Busyness is a powerful tool that works well in our nation. Prices are high and so many of the women have to work, leaving less time for the children. There isn't even time to cook. A lot of these emotions used to get worked out in housecleaning through scrubbing the floors or working in the fields. Now we keep a lot of our emotions locked inside, leaving us more vulnerable to the enemy than the people of former generations. Today we are very vulnerable to the enemy.

The enemy controls us tremendously through fear. Fear is probably the very bottom line of most of our emotions. Fear is where satan has the most control because it is the opposite of love. It causes us to doubt God's love for us, and yet the most powerful weapon that God has given to us is the gift of His love. The opposite of love is fear. Jesus tells us over and over, "Do not live in fear, little flock" (Lk 12:32). Once we're afraid, we're into the enemy's camp. We are vulnerable. We fear so many things that fear can become a stronghold within us.

Even the priest I mentioned earlier who came with severe depression and rage was affected by this fear. He was dealing with repressed anger from abuse in his childhood, but the underlying problem was his disbelief that God loved *him*. He had an underlying controlling spirit of fear moving within him. This priest was so scared of the Father in heaven, he was scared to death of Him, and satan was using that fear to magnify his doubt of God's love for him personally. So what we saw on the outside was a man in control: he tried to control his life, his prayer, he tried to control everything. This was his protection mechanism. Fear was the fig leaf that he kept putting on, and it was lurking down deep.

Sometimes in deliverance ministry and spiritual warfare we won't see the deepest root that is causing the problem. We might see the second, third, or fourth root, but we want to get to that bottom root. We want to get the whole plant uprooted. Sometimes the hurt is so deep and firmly rooted that we look at some of the other manifestations first. These manifestations are symptoms that alert us of a deeper problem. In this priest the very root of his problem was fear. He was scared to death of the Father, and satan loved to use this against him.

The following story also shows us how destructive fear can be. I was living in the backyard of a doctor's home. Another doctor in the city was dying of cancer. He had been through all the medical routes, and now as a last resort had asked this doctor friend of mine to pray over him. Doctors usually don't pray with doctors because they are very scientific, so this meant he was desperate. This doctor friend of mine came to me and asked, "I don't know what I should do. Do you think I should pray?" I said, "Why not?" "Well, it would take a miracle." "That's right. To whom else would you go for a miracle?" "But God doesn't do miracles anymore." "Well, do you want to see one?" "If I could see one, then maybe I could really believe." So we just left it at that, and I said, "Well, Lord, You know how to show him a miracle." I would think that every time this doctor delivered a baby he would be in awe of the miracle of life and would believe in miracles.

Anyway, we went to the prayer meeting early that night because I had been asked to pray with somebody before the prayer meeting. I didn't know anything about this person, just that he was passing through town. Normally we only pray with people after the prayer meeting, but they wanted me to pray with him before the meeting. This was a little unusual. I went in the back room and met a man about twenty years old who could not hear or speak, so we had to write notes to communicate. Now the obvious prayer would be to ask the Lord for him to be able to speak and hear, but I stopped and asked the Lord first, "Lord, how should we pray?" We always have to ask the Lord what His heart desires. We don't ever take anything for granted in the spiritual life.

The Lord said to pray for baptism. I thought "My, that's strange." My mind was racing, "Well, he's deaf and dumb. Who do I know in Omaha that can sign and give him instructions? What priest can we take him to?" I was thinking of the sacramental system of the Church. The Lord said, "No, pray right now for the Spirit to come upon him." So I wrote a little note and said, "Would you like to be baptized in the Holy Spirit and let God's love come upon you right now?" He just lit up; his face was radiant. He was saying yes. So that's all we did. We said a simple little prayer for the Holy Spirit to come, and that was it. It took about five minutes, and then we went into the prayer meeting. He was sitting next to me, and as we started singing praise music, all of a sudden he put his hand up to his throat like he was choking and gagging. He just looked terrified, and I thought, "Oh my goodness!" I put my hand on his shoulder, praying, "Lord, what's going on?" God said, "This is deliverance. Just let him know that it's all right. Reassure him that it will be over in a minute." And it was. The evil spirit of fear left him. This evil spirit of fear had paralyzed him as a two-year old child. Now God had delivered him, and he could speak, and he could hear! Isn't that beautiful?

On the way home that night there was silence in the car, and I said to my doctor friend, "Well, what do you think about miracles?" He said, "I think that we had better go pray with this doctor." So we did, and this doctor friend of mine laid hands on the other doctor, and he was totally healed of cancer.

The enemy would like us to think that he has more power than God does. He would like to paralyze us in fear. But the power comes through God's love. We can't say that an evil spirit lurks behind every person who is deaf or dumb, but when dealing with an individual, it doesn't hurt to bind the spirit of fear and any other spirit that may be present. It doesn't hurt to call forth God's love to fill the person up because what is there to lose? Maybe that person will hear. Maybe there is an evil spirit there. This is where the gift of discernment, the gift of being able to hear and follow God's mind and heart, comes in.

Always let the Lord have His way; ask Him what He wants to do. Satan lurks in our emotions and in our hearts. He's hiding. He's always in darkness and concealment, riding along in our emotions whenever we're not dealing with our feelings. We might not always deal with our own anger or unforgiveness, our sloth or depression, or any of our other emotions. When this happens, we are not whole, and these spirits can come right in.

So we need that helmet of salvation on, our deep belief that God loves *me*. If we find ourselves beginning to get discouraged and starting to go downhill, then we need to get in deeper touch with the Lord. We need to bring all our feelings into the light, to the One who is Light! It's all right to be angry, but it's not all right to stuff our anger and later end up exploding at people. We can always tell God if we're angry at Him. We need to go to Him and tell Him what's going on, or satan will tell us all kinds of lies as to why God doesn't love us. The helmet of salvation has to be firmly on. Yes, God does love me. Sometimes we deny that we're mad at God and may project our anger at other people who have nothing to do with it. The real problem is that there is something about God that we don't like or understand.

I remember when John F. Kennedy was assassinated. This was very upsetting to many of us, but then when Bobby Kennedy was killed some years later, I was angry at God. I remember storming into the chapel saying, "Lord, this is a bit much. If I were God, I wouldn't have let this happen." We might often say, "If I were God, I'd do it differently." You see, there are things about God and the way He does things or doesn't do things that we don't like. We need to be in touch with our feelings. If we aren't, these feelings can come out viciously against other people. They can manifest themselves within us and poison us.

Love, openness, and honesty are absolutely key to what we do with our emotions. When our emotions are high and we don't know what to do, we journal it out. We write it out. We write love letters to the Lord and get whatever is going on inside us out into the open. We talk about it with a confessor, significant other, and the Lord. We will begin going through the healing process so that door can be closed to all spirits other than the Holy Spirit.

The first stage in this healing process of our emotions is denial. If we deny that our feelings are hurt, "Well, it didn't bother me. It was just a little thing," then satan scoots right in. He loves these hidden hurt feelings. He hates littleness, but he'll use it on us to achieve his purposes. How many times have we said, "I don't think I'll say anything. It's so insignificant. It's so petty. It's so little." We will keep quiet until all these little things grow and grow until they have become a mountain. We won't be able to understand what's wrong with us anymore, but it's because there were so many things that we didn't handle.

So it's always good to journal our feelings out. "Lord, I'm upset. Did you hear what they said? I'm angry. What do You think about it?" We need to do whatever we can to begin releasing our emotions and bringing them into God's light and out of satan's territory. Satan operates like a bat. Bats can't see well in daylight. They bump into things in the daylight, but they do very well in the darkness. They do very well at night. So if we have a thought or emotion that we are hiding or stuffing, we shouldn't go into denial about it. We don't have to tell anyone about it, but we should tell it to the Lord. Like little children who go to mommy and daddy for everything, for every little owie to kiss it and make it better, we need to bring everything to the Father. It's just that simple. Our Abba will kiss it and all will be well.

Then we might go into the next stage of healing our emotions: "I shouldn't be feeling like this. After all, I'm a Christian." "I really should love everybody, after all, I'm a nun." "After all, God really has done so much for me." So we may deny our true feelings, thinking, "I'm not going to let this bother me. I'm really going to be big about it." We will be stuffing our true feelings deep inside, and through all this satan will be having a field day. Our feelings are being repressed. He is even using our desire to be good and holy to keep our true feelings hidden. He is busy working in the dark, in concealment. Hopefully we will decide to go to our Abba and tell Him what is going on so that our

83

helmet will be in place, and we will remain secure in the fact that God loves me.

If we get past this stage, we may go into another stage called bargaining. "Oh, Lord, I think I could forgive her if..." "In this situation You know I really can't forgive her because so all You have to do is touch her/his heart. Change her/him and everything will be fine." And we bargain!

I had a dear priest friend who was hard of hearing. He was retired but still wanted to hear confessions. This was going to be his service to the Church. He loved hearing confessions. So he went through the bargaining process. Jesus was Jewish so He's used to bargaining. He's good at bargaining Himself. We won't win. We'll never win. He always wins! So this priest was bargaining with the Lord, "If You heal me, I will hear confessions. There are not a lot of priests hearing confessions anymore. I can do this." Finally, one day the Lord did respond. He called this priest by name and said, "I will heal you, not because I need you, but because I love you." He did. God healed him.

When we get through this bargaining stage, our defenses are weakening, and we might go into depression. We have to be careful not to stop at this bargaining stage or we will go down and down and down. It can get awfully dark, and we can lose hope. We can become discouraged and even suicidal. There are many different levels, but once again if we can get our feelings and thoughts out to the Lord rather than keeping them inside, we will be okay. We can come out of a difficult situation stronger and into total acceptance of God's will. Then we give God the freedom to move in our lives in whatever way He wants to move. We can trust in Him and believe in His love for us.

I mentioned these emotional healings to show that inner healing doesn't happen all by itself. It doesn't always involve just our own feelings. Sometimes there are evil spirits hiding behind our hurt emotions and helping them along. We may need healing of our emotions and the binding and casting out of the evil ministering spirits. Deliverance ministry doesn't stand all by itself because people always need the unfailing love of God. Whatever has opened the door for those evil spirits to come in needs to be healed, and with God's help, the door will be closed. Deliverance and healing work side by side. They go together. This is true of any of the emotions.

We all deal with pride more than any other sin because pride is the father of all capital sins. The enemy is constantly getting to us through pride. We might not even recognize it. It might be that we need to be more submissive to authority, more open with the Lord, or more honest with those we live with. Pride might be preventing us from praying for people we don't like or praying for people who have hurt us. When we refuse to pray for anyone who is an enemy or has persecuted or hurt us in any way, we are manifesting pride. We are saying, "It's their fault. They're wrong. I don't need to be healed, they do." This may be our own human spirit and feelings of pride, but there is also an evil spirit of pride. We must be very careful to deal with our own human spirit and feelings of pride, closing the door to them. If we don't, the evil spirit of pride may come to help along our own pride, and we'll end up in dangerous spiritual waters.

We need to know ourselves. We need to be aware. We need self-knowledge. If we're tired, spirits can attack us more easily. They know when we're tired. We may be feeling that we need to spend more time in prayer. Maybe we are falling asleep in prayer but want to pray. So we take a step back and examine why we are falling asleep in prayer. Maybe we're not getting to bed on time so we need more sleep. That could be the door letting these spirits in to block our real desire to pray. We can resolve to close this door to tiredness because we can see the enemy working through our tiredness and fatigue. So we make sure that we get to bed on time. There are high-powered spirits of fatigue. When we are tired and fatigued, all our emotions go haywire. It's easier to get angry. We can get upset and blow things out of proportion. Little problems can get magnified, and there can be a lot of bad fruit. So we simply close the door, lay the ax to the root of the problem, and see to it that we get sufficient rest. It can be just that simple.

It's a process. Begin with whatever the symptom is and start backing up. It's a little bit difficult to speak generally on this because each person is different, but the process that we use is, "This is how I'm acting and overreacting. Why?" Usually we don't know the why right away. We don't know why that statement bothered us. We don't know why all of a sudden we became angry. We just did. Something was triggered within us so we ask God for help, "Show me what's going on inside of me." We don't have to figure out everything that's going on inside of us. We have the Spirit of Truth. He's already there. We have the Spirit of Light. He wants to help us. We have divine help at all times ready to show us, if we simply ask. It's all in our asking.

There are many ways to pray for help. Again, we have to seek God's mind about how to pray. Once He shows us His mind, this is the area in which God is going to move. It could be that God would have us pray for a desire to want to pray in the first place. Often when we are not taking the time to pray, the first thing we say is, "Well, I'm so busy. I don't have this kind of time to pray. If I take time to pray, my ministry is going to suffer. I've got to be here, I've got to be there." But if you process it through, often the reason that we don't pray is not that I'm not taking the time or that I don't have the time. The reason that we don't pray is because it is not a priority. The reason that praying is not a priority is because I don't have the desire to pray. We have to be honest with ourselves. Maybe we don't pray because our prayer seems dry and boring, and we can't wait to get it over with. Nothing seems to be happening. If this is true, it is going to be easy to skip prayer. So we have to question and see the desires of our hearts. Oftentimes this is where God will start.

Once a woman came and said, "I cannot forgive. I absolutely cannot forgive." Now we always used to think, "You've got to forgive. You've got to forgive." We have learned that this is not always the first step. Jesus showed me her heart. Her heart was absolutely filled with thorns, pierced with pain, and He said, "Let's remove some of this pain first." A person can't forgive when they're in this kind of pain. They need to be loved first. When we can be loved and begin to be healed, then we can forgive. So forgiveness is not always the very first step. Otherwise, the next day the hurt and pain will be back because the door was never closed.

As long as we stuff all our emotions and feelings and have this garbage within us, the rats will come. That's exactly what we're doing. We actually can feed these evil spirits. They are very much at home in darkness and with garbage. Darkness and garbage are not the food that the Lamb of God has for us at all. So we have to be careful not to let satan get into our mind. This is the area he breaks through better than any other area. As prayer warriors, we can have all of the armor on, including the shield of faith and the sword, but if our head is not protected, we don't stand a chance out there in the battle. The attack comes in the mind. It comes very easily in the Western Church because we are very scientific. We are more left-brained. Everything about the mind is very important to us, with all of our degrees and everything. So we have to be very careful because this is where we are letting the enemy come in.

Therefore, "**Take the helmet of salvation**" (Eph 6:17) and put on the mind of Jesus Christ. Our thoughts must be deeply rooted in faith and hope in His great love for us!

Chapter 5

The Breastplate of Righteousness

"Stand fast, with . . . righteousness
as your breastplate."
Eph 6:14

The breastplate covers an extremely important area: the heart. If an arrow shoots through the breastplate into the heart, that could be it. So much of the armor goes along with the Beatitudes. The breastplate of righteousness coincides with, "Blessed are the single-hearted for they shall see God" (Mt 5:8). Those with a pure heart shall see God! We need this union with God. Every prayer warrior wants to see God. Every prayer warrior needs to see God. With this purity of heart our breastplate will be in place, covering our heart that is pure. The heart is so precious. We must always keep it pure and protected.

One time I asked the Lord, "Why did You hold up a child as our model of sanctity?" Have you ever thought about that? Why a child? Thank goodness it was a child! Imagine how difficult it would be if He had held up a great leader, somebody who would have been almost impossible for us to imitate! Instead He brings forth a little child. A child is our model of sanctity. God answered my question, "Unless you change and become a little child, you cannot enter the kingdom of heaven" (Mk 10:15; Lk 18:17). So I asked Him, "Why a little child?" He simply said, "Because babies don't sin." Babies are pure.

The Lord is after the pure of heart. He wants our hearts to be pure, to be full of love, to be full of His love. I used to wonder what it meant to be a saint. A priest often gave me the words, "Lord, make me a saint" for my penance. Saint Claude de Colombiere used to pray, "Make me a saint in spite of myself." I like this prayer! So I thought, "What in the world is a saint?" We all have different concepts of what a saint is. St. Paul says that a saint is someone who is full of God's love. It's not difficult to be full of God's love, but it *is* difficult to get rid of our self-love. This can be painful and crucifying at times because it means something in us has to die. Something has to go so that Someone greater can live in its place. St. John the Baptist knew this and said, "He must increase, while I must decrease" (Jn 3:30). One translation that I love says, "He must increase and I must disappear." We must lose our selves and disappear into Jesus. We must take on His mind and His heart and become one with Him.

So this breastplate of righteousness requires purity of heart. The only way this is possible is through transforming union, where we become one with God. We might say it's an exchange of our heart for His heart. In the Christmas liturgy we pray, "O wondrous exchange." This is it: Divinity takes on our humanity, and our humanity is exchanged for His Divinity. We certainly got the better part here! It is a beautiful exchange of His love for our sinfulness. Whenever we discuss anything about the heart, it always has to do with love; they are one and the same. Those who love much will have a pure heart. They will pray much because they will want to be with the person they love so much. So as we are drawn into this transforming union, our hearts will become more pure, and we will want to spend all our time in union with God. It's just that simple. When we love, we will always find time to pray, a place to pray, and different ways to pray.

There are as many different ways to pray as there are different ways to love. Love is creative. We don't really have to be taught how to pray because we don't really have to be taught how to love. It is pure gift. When we love, we know how to respond to that person because their cares and concerns are ours also. We need to know that God is asking us to let Him love us. He is in love with us, and He wants us to be in love with Him as well. This is where purity of heart comes in. We'll start to seek the exchanging our heart for God's heart. We'll start to understand God better because we'll be in union with Him. We will have His heart. We'll start to constantly check things out with God first because discernment will become our way of life. We will only want to do things God's way. The pure of heart can discern well because they can see God. God is the discerner. Discernment is not of the mind; it's of the heart. It's the heart that sees, hears, and knows. God is love. God is a heart Person, and He communicates with us Heart to heart. It's really beautiful to have a relationship with the Lord.

So this breastplate of righteousness is saying that things have to be right with the Lord. It's not self-righteousness. It's His will, not ours. It's surrender to Him. It's letting go of our agendas, our concepts, and our ideas in exchange for His. It's becoming more and more flexible so that when something doesn't go our way, we don't get so upset. Not that that would happen to us! I love the story of Zaccheus. I can really identify with him because he's little. He's so little! There were so many people around that Zaccheus had to climb a tree to see Jesus. Jesus obviously had gained a large following by now. There was no way Zaccheus would be able to see Jesus unless he climbed a tree because he was small of stature and because of the crowd. Zaccheus climbed the sycamore tree, and Jesus came to the very spot where Zaccheus was. Can't you just see this little guy up there hanging out of the tree trying to look down? Jesus looked up and said, "Zaccheus, hurry down. I mean to stay at your house today" (Lk 19:5). Isn't that beautiful? Hurry down. Hurry!

God is calling us to hurry; He wants to stay at our house today! We are a house of God. We are His temple. He wants us to come down and go deep within to where He is waiting for us. He wants to be at home in us and enter into a deeper friendship with us. Zaccheus's response is beautiful! "He quickly descended" (Lk 19:6). So many times we think, "If I'm going to be a saint, if I'm going to be close to God, I've got to be perfect. I've got to be so good. I've got to go to the heights." We can go to the heights if the eagle, the Spirit of God, takes us to the heights. Otherwise, we just go down deep within ourselves to where God is always waiting for us. "He quickly descended and welcomed Jesus with delight" (Lk 19:6).

Now everybody starts to murmur, "He has gone to a sinner's house as a guest" (Lk 19:7). We may experience these same feelings when we watch people go to Communion. We can almost say along with the crowd, "Oh my goodness, Lord, You're coming into a sinner's house." And He is. We are redeemed sinners. We are saved sinners, but we still sin every day. If the just man falls seven times, what about us? God loves sinners. Jesus' whole mission is for people like us. It's all right with the Lord that we're not perfect. Satan would try to have us think that we have to have our act together before we go to the Lord. He wants us to think that once we've sinned there isn't any way for us to return to the Lord. Look at how we try to conceal something even in the confessional! We may pass over a particular sin quickly so that maybe God will hear, but the priest won't. We need to have things out in the open, especially when we're involved with God. We want our heart to be right with God. We want to be pure.

One of the main things I love about the Catholic Church is that it's a Church full of sinners. This was my ticket in! God loves sinners. He loves sinners. He wanted to come to Zaccheus's house as a guest, and Zaccheus wanted to make things right. So this is what we do. If we love the Lord, we always want to make things right with Him. If we want Him to remain with us, we don't want anything at all to come between us, nothing. Anything we conceal, minimize, or withhold can compromise our relationship and allow all these little footholds for the enemy to come in. We may end up becoming self-righteous, not righteous in the Lord. This is not the breastplate for the warrior. We want God's righteousness, not our self-righteousness. God alone is the righteous One.

Once while driving into Lourdes, everyone was in prayer and deep in their own thoughts. The five of us in the car were silent. I was driving, and I realized that deep within me I was saying something. I really didn't know what I was saying because I was speaking in Latin, and I don't know Latin. I kept repeating this phrase, and it was going to the rhythm of the click-click-click of the tires. I was saying, "Sed libera nos amalo, sed libera nos amalo" all the way into Lourdes. Later I found out that it meant, "deliver us from evil." I thought it was strange for me to get "deliver us from evil" because we were going to a holy place. I think of Lourdes as a healing place, with the healing water, Our Lady of Lourdes, the Immaculate Conception. As I pondered this, I began to see that the evil God wants us to be delivered from is sin. No wonder Mary came as the Immaculate Conception, this blessed, pure woman, to help free us from sin. She is calling us to be healed of sin, to be free of sin. She wants us to have this breastplate of righteousness, to be right before the Lord, to be in union with God. Mary wants us to be delivered from the evil one and from all the sin and tools which he uses to entice and tempt us.

Healing can take place at a deeper level, particularly in the Sacrament of Reconciliation, the beautiful gift God has given to the Catholic Church. Many of us who are converts have not had this sacrament all of our lives, and we cherish it very, very much. We always want to make sure things are right with the Lord. Perfect peace can only be found in His will, and cleansing our soul will bring us to this peace.

Satan can camouflage all our human emotions except one: he cannot camouflage joy. He can camouflage peace at different levels, but there is never a deception with joy. When we are in God's perfect will, even when His will is difficult, painful, and sacrificial, there can still be a joy that comes with another level of peace. Joy can flood our souls and bring us into a deeper union because we are so one with the heart of God. We can experience many camouflaged fruits of the enemy but he cannot camouflage joy. Joy is the infallible sign of the presence of God.

So anytime we are compromising, anytime we are trying to slide one by, anytime we are trying to shade things to make it not seem so bad, we need to be careful. We don't want to protect our faults; we want them to be exposed and healed. As God's light gets stronger inside us, we will see a lot of ways we have compromised without even knowing it. For example, I had a friend say to me, "It was just a little white lie." There isn't any such thing as a "white lie." A lie is a lie, and it's not of God no matter how little the lie may be. I used to exaggerate a lot. "I've told you a hundred thousand times." I find I'm more careful about my exaggerations because when I'm shading things, I'm not really speaking truth. I didn't realize this about exaggeration for a long time. There are so many ways the Lord will begin to show us where we need to grow. He will start to caution us, "Be careful of what you say. Is this perfect truth as you understand it?"

Remember we are always changing. We won't be the same people in a year as we are today. We may find that many of the things we think or say today, we will no longer believe in a year from now because we will have grown in knowledge and wisdom. Our position on certain issues may even have changed. That doesn't mean that a year ago we lied or that we're terrible. We shouldn't let satan come and attack us in this way. At the time, we spoke truth as fully as we knew it. So don't let satan condemn you.

Condemnation is one of satan's tools to always make us think less of ourselves. God will always build us up, and satan will always try to take us down. It's that simple. So we need this constant conversion process. We need to constantly become more pure of heart because Jesus has challenged us, "Babies don't sin." We're in this deeper union with Him, and that means we're like the Lamb of God. "Behold the Lamb," the vulnerable, weak little Lamb who takes away the sin of the world. Let Him take away the sin in you. Allow Him to place a pure breastplate over your heart.

We are always engaged in warfare and in prayer, always wanting the Lamb to use us to take away sin. Sin is everywhere: sins of abortion, sins of uncharitableness, and sins of greed, lust, and riches. But at the same time we must be sure to allow the Lamb to take away the sin in us, also. Sin can build very gradually and imperceptibly within us at times. As we become more purified ourselves, we will discover a deeper level of our own sin and our own sinfulness. Prayer warriors can begin to focus so much on other people's bondage, the nation's bondage, and the Church's bondage that we may find that we don't even realize that we're in bondage ourselves.

A simple way to help us to discover our sins is to look at our gifts. We all have gifts. Some have many while others have a few, but we all have gifts. We should look at our strengths and blessings. What do we consider as something that God has given to us that is just pure gift? Then look at the way we use that gift. Look at the way we may misuse or even abuse that gift. This is a good examination of conscience tool that will help us discover our sins before we go to confession. Sometimes we can't see the sin because we don't want to see the sin. Maybe we never thought of it as sin. We may not recognize sin as sin.

Once we were having a big ecumenical conference here in Omaha, and I somehow ended up being the facilitator of the entire operation. The Catholic Church was involved along with other denominations. It meant we were busy meeting with priests and ministers constantly, week after week, setting the details of this huge conference. It took about six months of preparation and work. It was a constant tug of war getting priests and ministers to organize and pull their own parishes and churches together.

Being an organizer is not one of my main gifts, so it was extremely difficult for me to try to organize all of this. I found as the days and weeks went by, I was getting tired and becoming more masculine, leaving my whole femininity behind. Men are supposed to be men, and they're beautiful when they're men. Women are beautiful when they're women. But when women cross over and start to take on the role of men, it's not beautiful anymore.

So this is where I was when I first heard this teaching on sin. The question that was put before all of us was, "What do you consider the best gift that God has given to you?" I was thinking of some of the gifts and thought, "I think the gift that He's given me that I love the most is that He made me a woman. I love being female." That's what I had on my mind. Then a few minutes later, the teacher said, "Now look at how you have misused and abused that gift." Well, I was horrified because I knew immediately that I had moved into a masculine role. I knew it: I was abusing my femininity. I was abusing everything I stood for, and I knew this was sin for me. Now I understood why things weren't going well. People were yelling at each other, and I didn't know what to do.

So I went to Confession and told Father, "I have sinned against my femininity. I'm not even in a woman's role right now." I could see this sin now, but I could only see it in the light of the gift. I never would have known what was going on if I hadn't first looked at the gift. So this beautiful priest said, "Let's just ask the Lord to send you a man to facilitate all of this or to help you." So we did, and the next day a friend called and asked, "How are you?" I said, "I'm just fine. Why do you ask?" He said, "Well, that's not what the Lord said." "Oh, really? What did He say?" "He said that you were not fine at all and I should call and see if you needed any help." "Help!" So he got out the job description, you know how men are just born organizers and facilitators, and he took the whole thing over. I went back into the things I could do: my role of inspiring, affirming, and nurturing. The conference was a great success. Eleven thousand people came and it bore much fruit. Looking at our gift is one way we can find our sin.

There are many ways to discover our sin. For example, our state in life dictates much of what we should or should not be doing. My state in life says that I have a call to pray. I have a responsibility to pray. Several years ago I was reading I Samuel 12:23 where Samuel was convicted by God of his prayerlessness. As I read this, I felt that same conviction deep within. I thought, "Oh my goodness. I should be praying a lot more than I am." I should be, you know, I'm in this full time. So I went to confession. "Father, I am sinning against my whole vocation of prayer. God is calling me to so much more."

So a lot depends on what gift He has given to us as individuals. He has given me a vocational gift to pray. I was starting to get too busy, so the Lord stopped me and reminded me through the prophet Samuel. Sin can happen in many ways, but it will happen where the gift is; it will be the flip side of the gift. That's why sinner and saint are the same; the flip side of the saint is the sinner, but hopefully for all of us, the flip side of the sinner is a future saint! So as we look at our sins, we must remember there's a saint in the making here.

Another point of discernment is that once we get the light and make a decision, the temptation will come from the enemy to change that decision. This temptation can come in many different ways and will often come when things get pretty stormy. It can come when it doesn't look like we made a good decision because all of a sudden, things aren't going right or going according to how we think they should be going. St. Ignatius Loyola, the founder of the Jesuits, cautions us here, "In time of desolation we should never make any change, but remain firm and constant" (*The Spiritual Exercises of St. Ignatius,* 318). Never, never turn the ship around in the middle of the storm. We are to never change our discernment while it's stormy. When we are at peace, when we are calm within ourselves, we may find then that we need to change course. We may find it wasn't the best discernment and that we need to re-discern because the enemy is involved somewhere, and it's not bearing good fruit. Don't be afraid to make that change and re-discern. When there's peace within us again, nine times out of ten we will know that we're right on course. We would not have wanted to change our course in the storm only to find we were on the right track initially.

For example, if we are angry, satan would like us to call up that person we are angry with right then and there to get this talked about. This is not a good time because we are not at peace. There is a justified anger that comes from the Holy Spirit; it's a controlled anger. If it's our own emotional anger, we may not have the control, and then we may strike out, causing hurt and further division. Many things could happen when we are getting into uncharted waters during the storm. So we must be careful of what we say and how we move, especially when we don't have peace. We always have to wait until we can shift back into neutral, into peace. We need the breastplate of righteousness firmly in place. Then the fruit will always be peace. We wait for that little peace branch to come back. We wait for the Dove to bring it back into our hearts. We don't want to get into enemy territory.

There are a few little guidelines about consolation and desolation that are helpful to know because they are tools of God, but they can also be used by the enemy. Desolation is always from the enemy, and its effect will always take us further away from God. Consolation will always bring us closer to God.

Sometimes we recognize desolation when we're really despondent, but we need to spot it before we get dragged to the bottom. Here are some manifestations of desolation: negativity, discouragement, self-pity, anxiety, turmoil, restlessness, impatience, tepidity, and complaining. Negative feelings are dangerous; they are not of God and can lead to deep desolation. These are not of God, and we need to come against them.

Discouragement is another manifestation of desolation and will draw us to the belief that maybe God doesn't love us or that God has abandoned us. We have to be careful here. It can lead to self-pity because in desolation all of a sudden the focus changes to myself. We are in dangerous spiritual waters when this happens. We need to focus totally on the Lord. When we start to focus on ourselves, self-pity can come and bring sadness with it. St.Teresa of Avila used to say, "God, deliver me from frowning saints." Sadness is not of God, so if we recognize these things happening within ourselves, we know that the enemy is working.

The enemy can use good things to destroy us. He can use our devotions and pious practices. I've seen people at prayer. It looks good, but if we speak to them or disturb them in any way, they become very upset. Look at the fruit. For heaven's sake, don't sit in their church pew! We can see spirits are working here, using good people who are doing what we would say are good things.

Fear is also one of satan's main tools. When we're afraid, we're not going to focus on the Lord. We lose our peace, get anxious, can become angry, upset, and unkind. The bottom line is that we're going to violate charity, the commandment of Jesus to love one another as He has loved us.

All of this is opposed to the personality of the Lamb. The Lamb is meek, the Lamb is humble, the Lamb is gentle. Jesus is everything satan is not; they are totally opposite. So we need to fight against this, particularly if we have developed habits. It takes time to develop a habit, good or bad. As we become aware of our bad habits, with the grace of God, we can move very easily into developing good habits. It really doesn't take that long to develop good habits once we become aware of it, examine our motives and our actions, and decide to change. We have to take a look at ourselves, as well, to see why we are acting or reacting the way that we are.

Sadness and unrest come from the enemy. Remember the rich young man? "He went away sad, for he had many possessions" (Mk 10:22). He was saddened. He wasn't ready to leave his earthly treasures behind. Sorrow and sadness are not the same thing. We can see the difference when we look at the fruit or the results from a particular attitude or situation. Jesus said, "You can tell a tree by its fruit" (see Mt 7:20; Mt 12:33). Sadness will lead us into depression and self-pity; these are not of God.

On the other hand, sorrow is healthy and produces deeper love and understanding. It causes spiritual growth and calls us to action. Jesus said, "My heart is filled with sorrow to the point of death" (Mk 14:34). The heart of

Jesus sorrowed, and ours will, too, if we remain with the heart of Jesus. We have to allow for grieving time, for that pain. There are a lot of people today who are in sorrow over all the abortions, the loss of precious babies. There is a lot of sorrow over the things going on in Rwanda. Sorrow is not of the enemy, for it produces good fruit. Sorrow is of God. Sorrow and joy live side by side in the soul. There is no conflict there. If we watch the fruit, we'll be able to tell.

A thought can also be known by its fruit. What kind of fruit is this thought producing within us? Then we can tell pretty much who is behind this particular thought. We have to watch carefully over our thought life. If we feel some sadness or unrest about a decision we have made, feel free to re-discern it. It's okay to make a mistake. We are human and are limited, so we're going to make a lot of mistakes. But don't deny the mistakes or pretend that they're not there, for to build one mistake upon another would be foolish. Rather, we need to go back and re-discern our thoughts or decisions right away and tell the Lord about our mistakes. It's okay. This is humility and it's dealing with truth. Whenever we walk in truth, we walk in freedom. Satan cannot touch us when we're in that freedom and light.

Once again we go back to the image of the child because a child is free. Children are not perfect in the sense of doing perfect things. The spirit of perfection that many of us have is not of God. God alone is the perfect One. Children are imperfect. They really don't do anything well; they don't do everything right. They're little. They do the best they can. That's all God asks of us: that we do the best we can, but it isn't going to be perfect. We're going to fall into the mud puddles. We're going to disobey, but when this happens with our own children, we don't love them any less. No, we put them in the bathtub, clean them up, and discipline them, "Don't do this again." But we don't stop loving them. God *never* stops loving us. He's calling us to this union. This is important for prayer warriors more than ever before: we must exchange our heart for His heart, we must move in His perfect will. Satan cannot break through and attack us when we're in that kind of union.

So don't hide from the Lord. Whatever we do, don't hide from the Lord. Always go back to Genesis 3 to see the personality of satan and his tactics. It's all there. Adam and Eve hid. They hid, and our all-knowing, all-loving God said, "Where are you?" (Gn 3:9) We have to remember that if we keep hiding, we're not going to know ourselves or who we are. So never hide from the Lord. We have many mechanisms for running and for hiding: busyness, talking on the phone a lot, watching TV, reading good books, whatever; anything to avoid prayer, anything to avoid that face to face dialogue meeting with the Lord. We know what are own personal ways of running and hiding. We have all sorts of ways of avoiding Him. So we must be careful that we're not running or hiding from the Lord.

Whenever we do workshops on spiritual warfare, we get a lot of questions about people who are mentally ill, particularly schizophrenia. I'm not saying that everyone who is diagnosed schizophrenic has an evil spirit, but I want to share how evil spirits work because often there are spirits involved in mental illness. When we can bind the evil spirits and subdue them in mentally ill people, often the healing that needs to take place can happen so much more quickly than through medical science. This has happened to us many times in intercessory prayer and many times in one-on-one ministry.

There was a woman brought to us who was diagnosed as schizophrenic. I knew her psychiatrist and the priest who were working with her. The three of us teamed up to help her. The first thing we did was get rid of these spirits that were harassing her and giving her dual personalities. I was waiting for the anointing of the Holy Spirit to come to throw out these spirits, but it didn't happen. So I said, "Lord, where are You?" because all the spirits were bound and everything was ready. He said, "Leave them be. We're not going to cast them out right now because we cannot strip her of the only personality she knows. So just keep binding these spirits. Build her up with Me, with Scriptures, with love, with prayer. When the time is right and her personality is adhered to the personality of Jesus in this beautiful breastplate of righteousness, then it will be time to cast these spirits out. When her spirit is adhered to mine, she will be fine. She won't miss these other personalities because she will have a personality with Me." And that's what we did. Every day we would take authority over these spirits and bind them. She never knew what we did, day after day. After a year, the Lord said, "Now is the time." It was an official exorcism that took place in a church here with our official Church exorcist. Satan was cast out, and she was so built up in the Lord that she was fine. She is a very strong Christian, and works for the pro-life cause today, and is a beautiful, beautiful person.

God works slowly, always respecting the dignity of the person. He loves us. He desires that we remain pure in Him. He wants us to take precious care of our heart. He wants us to belong only to Him. This is our area of greatest protection: our unity with the Father. So **"Stand fast, with . . . righteousness as your breastplate"** (Eph 6:14) for the Lord desires to work through us. We have already been given so many weapons to protect us and help us to stand fast!

Chapter 6

Draw Your Strength
From the Lord

"Draw your strength from the Lord
and from His mighty power."
Eph 6:10

When we think about the armor, we can recall the helmet, breastplate, and shield, but no matter how fully clothed we are or how many weapons we have, if we don't have the strength and the power of the Lord, we are not going to win the battle. We won't even dare to step forward onto the front lines. Prayer warriors are in the vanguard of the Church as specialized units, like the Green Berets, who get sent in first.

So we have to be prepared. We have to be out there in strength, but we are so very little. We can't do this by ourselves. This is key because when we are weak, it's only then that we are strong (2 Cor 12:10). Only the little ones call on God for His strength. So in order to fight these kinds of spirits, this kind of evil, we need God's strength. These spirits are extremely intelligent, strong, and powerful. They have knowledge far beyond our own. They are spirits. It would be so foolish and deadly for us to try to go into enemy territory without the strength and the power of the Lord.

St. Paul prayed, "For this reason I kneel before the Father, from whom every family in heaven and on earth is named, that he may grant you in accord with the riches of his glory to be strengthened with power through his Spirit in the inner self" (Eph 3:14-16). It's the Spirit who gives us our strength. St. Paul also prayed, "May He enlighten your innermost vision that you may know the great hope to which He has called you, the wealth of His glorious heritage to be distributed among the members of the Church and the immeasurable scope of His power in us who believe" (Eph 1:18-19). This power is the same power which He showed us when He raised Christ from the dead and seated Him at His right hand in heaven. This is tremendous strength, and it comes especially from the Holy Spirit.

We see this at Pentecost. The Church itself wasn't engaged in the battle. They weren't ready yet. It was Jesus who was in battle. He had the strength. He had the power. He is the strength. Yet after the descent of the Holy Spirit when the Church received this power, then we see the Church engaged in battle. There are harassment, killings, and crucifixions, and it was during this battle that evangelization was at its best. This could happen because they were prepared now. They had been told to wait there in Jerusalem until they were "Clothed with power from on high" (Lk 24:49). This is the same thing we do as prayer warriors: we wait until we are clothed with power from on high, and then, and only then, we go forth.

Just because we are in high-powered ministry and have been clothed with the power and strength of the Holy Spirit, it doesn't mean that we are ready for the next time. We constantly wait upon the Lord for that fresh outpouring, that new anointing, that green light. We always wait for the strength of the Holy Spirit and His permission to take on the enemy again in whatever way that God is showing us. We need His power; we need His strength. We need to be in a posture like the apostles and Our Lady were in: waiting, open, and expecting the outpouring of the Holy Spirit. We, too, need the Upper Room experience every day. Once isn't enough. Just like it isn't enough to have a wonderful Thanksgiving dinner and then hold true to our claim, "I'm never going to eat again." We need constant nourishment from the Holy Spirit to be filled and strengthened.

Sometimes we can receive so much from God that we think it's enough, but it will never be enough. Scripture tells us, "Blest are they who hunger and thirst for holiness; they shall have their fill" (Mt 5:6). We will always thirst because that's how God is enticing us, always luring us to come for more, to constantly be refilled. If our energies are constantly going forth in this battle, in warfare, in ministries, in loving, and in giving, then we have to be filled ourselves. We have to constantly be receiving. We can't give something we don't have. It's that simple.

In the Bible story of the woman and the dragon we see this need to constantly be filled. "She gave birth to a son . . . The woman herself fled into the desert, where a special place had been prepared for her by God. The woman was given the wings of a gigantic eagle so that she could fly off to her place in the desert" (Rv 12:5,6,14). The eagle is a symbol of contemplative spirituality. John the Beloved, the evangelist, is always symbolized as the eagle because he rested and leaned upon the heart of Jesus. He knew how to listen. He knew how to receive, and in this kind of love, he was lifted right up into the heart of God. Contemplative spirituality is resting upon and being lifted into the heart of Jesus. We don't say much; not that we can't speak, but the emphasis is on receiving. It's on listening. It's on experiencing.

St. Paul said, "May He strengthen you inwardly through the working of His Spirit. May Christ dwell in your hearts through faith, and may charity be the root and foundation of

105

your life. Thus you will be able to grasp fully, with all the holy ones, the breadth and length and height and depth of Christ's love, and experience this love which surpasses all knowledge, so that you may attain to the fullness of God Himself" (Eph 3:16-19). This is the very heart of contemplative spirituality: to experience the love that comes from the heart of God. This is what God wants. This is where we get our strength. There is nothing as strong as love. When we are loved, we're happy, "for rejoicing in the Lord must be your strength" (Neh 8:10). It's the song that we sing: "The joy of the Lord is our strength." Joy is the fruit of that love.

This is why we see all this joy at Pentecost. They were being loved as they had never been loved before. The Holy Spirit was pouring forth, filling them with God's love. The great Gift of Love was coming upon them in such plenitude that people thought they were intoxicated. Well, they were! They were filled with Love, with the New Wine. John of the Cross refers to this as going down into the wine cellar and drinking deeply of Love. That's joy! That's pure homecoming! This is where the strength and the energy come. It's the Holy Spirit who energizes us. He is uncreated energy. He is power. So when we are filled with God's love, it is then that we are strong because it's His love that is permeating and filling us. This joy of the Lord pours forth, we are in union with God, and we are strong now.

There comes a time when we can't share the experience. St. Paul was a great missionary and mystic, but he couldn't share this kind of experience. All he could do now was to pray that all of us would have it. We can't share an experience of our own with anybody. One of the symbols I use a lot is the orange. We could teach about where the oranges grow best, what kind of climate they need, when they should be picked, and how they should be processed. We could discuss the vitamins developed

106

within it and about how good it is for us to eat an orange. But there is no way we can convey what an orange really tastes like to anyone. We must try it ourselves; it has to be our own personal experience. We don't personally know anyone unless we are experiencing that person.

I used to hear wonderful things about Pope John Paul. I would even see him on television, but it wasn't until I stood in St. Peter's Square, and he came out in that little Popemobile that the spirit of the man, the personality of the man, the holiness, the office, the Vicar of Christ, that I experienced the Holy Father. All of a sudden I was having an experience of John Paul, and no matter how hard I can try to relay that to anyone, the depth is missing. We have to experience him personally to understand. Likewise, no one can share fully with another what God really tastes like, what He feels like, and what He is like. We have to have our own personal experience of Him.

I used to wonder why people would go to apparition sites or charismatic conferences. Then they'd come to the cloister and try to share it with us, but words were never sufficient. Frustrated they would say, "Well, you just should have been there. It was wonderful. Oh, it was just the greatest ever." Thirty minutes later, we still knew nothing because it was their experience, and they couldn't share the depth of it. There are no words for experience. It has to be experienced personally. God is calling each of us personally to this kind of prayer. Those of us on the front lines, who are going more and more into the enemy's camp, need the depth of this experience to receive the strength and power of God.

Satan will always strike at those who are on the front lines. He's always trying to divide a soul from God. There are all sorts of ways he uses, such as trying to tell us we are somebody other than who we really are and putting us down all the time. However, when we're in this kind of union, he can't successfully do this because we know who we are. We've begun to know who God is, and we will be strong from this union. In Jewish terminology, knowledge means to experience someone. When Mary said to the angel, "How can this be since I do not know man?" (Lk 1:34), she was saying "I have not *experienced* man." There's a beautiful Scripture in the Old Testament, "For it is love that I desire, not sacrifice, and knowledge of God rather than holocausts" (Hos 6:6). God is saying, "I want love. I want you to experience Me." We can take that a step further and answer with Mary, "But I don't know who You are." God keeps encouraging us, "Seek and you will find. Knock and it will be opened to you" (Mt 7:7). There is always a deeper level of God to experience, and all He is asking us to do is to try to know Him. He wants us to take one little baby step at a time and experience Him.

Have you ever played hide and seek with children? Children can't really find an adult because an adult can outthink them, outsmart them, and out-hide them. So we play to bring pleasure to the child. We hide and then kind of clear our throats, rustle the leaves, cough, or knock something over to help them out. Then they say, "I found you. I found you." What joy it brings to their hearts to find us. That's what God does with us, too. He lets us find Him, but really it is He who reveals Himself to us. We could never find Him on our own. It's all pure gift. It's all revelation and as we seek, He will reveal Himself. All He asks is for us to desire to know Him.

Contemplative spirituality is pure gift. It is gift of God. All we need to do is want it, desire it, and ask for it because this is what He wants. St. Paul tells us God's perfect will for us is to "attain the fullness of God Himself" (Eph 3:19). His perfect will is not for us to be giving Him something, not even giving Him souls or fighting the war. His first perfect will for us is receiving deeply of Himself. He desires this because He is Love. Love always has more to give. Love always seeks union. God is waiting for us to look for Him so He can reveal Himself to us.

We need to be like the stars. When the stars were created by God, He spoke to them, and they responded, "Here we are!" (Bar 3:34-35) I love that, "Here we are." Likewise, we can say, "Here I am, Lord. I'm just waiting for You. You are the God that comes." This is what happens in prayer every day. Union with God has nothing to do with ministry. We have it all wrong; we think it's something we do. Rather it is God who ministers to us. God is the initiator; we are not. Together, we, the Church, are the Bride of Christ, and it's the Bridegroom who initiates union. Love Himself initiates union. He seeks us, and all we can do is say, "Here I am Lord. I'm waiting for You. I'm available to You."

Once we enter deeply into this kind of prayer those eagle wings lift us up. The eagle is a beautiful symbol of contemplative spirituality because eagles fly straight to the sun. They live in high places. We don't normally have eagles around Omaha, Nebraska, but for some reason about five years ago they showed up at Bellwether, and they stayed. We got so excited! We went running out, "Oh, look! Oh, look! Oh, look!" Another beautiful thing about eagles are the little eaglets. They're up high in the nest. It's very comfortable, cozy, and warm up there in the nest, so what does the mother eagle do when her little ones won't leave the nest? She starts picking away the nest. She takes the nest away and all of a sudden, the eaglets are forced to fly. They can't fly as of yet so they start to drop, but she gets under them, and they light on her back. Mama eagle takes them back up to the nest and pushes them off again. All the while she's right there under them. It's a beautiful thing how they are taught to fly.

Like the eaglets, we can get very comfortable up there on the high places with the mother eagle. But all of a sudden, we'll start to get disturbed and will think, "Oh, my goodness. Something's wrong with my prayer. It's not so comfy and cozy anymore." Maybe there is something wrong but probably not. The Holy Spirit Himself can disturb us even in the high places because He wants us to go higher. He wants to teach us. It's in the struggle that we learn to fly. This is how we learn to soar.

Eagles don't flap their wings; the wind carries them. They know how to ride the wind. This is how we can distinguish eagles from other birds. The other birds are using their wings, flapping away, and expending their energy. In the earlier stages of prayer, we, too, may flap our wings. Sometimes it seems like we have to put forth a lot of energy to even understand a word of Scripture. It may be difficult just to get into prayer, to quiet ourselves, but there will come a breakthrough. It will come. All of a sudden, we won't be flapping our wings to travel even the distance. We will soar on the wind of the Spirit! The Breath of God will carry us, and we will rest. Contemplative spirituality is resting in the Lord. It is refreshing because we are receiving. Many other things are happening while we are soaring. Our eyes will be opened and the gifts of the Holy Spirit will start to operate. The Holy Spirit will be very active within us and the gift of Wisdom will start to operate at a deeper level. We will start seeing things more from God's point of view, literally a bird's-eye view. We won't be looking up from our sheltered, very narrow state anymore, but we will start seeing more of a panoramic view like what God sees.

This is important for prayer warriors. We have to see. We have to gaze with God's eyes. He wants us to know as He knows. "Indeed, the Lord God does nothing without revealing His plan to His servants" (Am 3:7). He wants us to know as He knows because this will influence all our actions. Our prayer and our mission will truly become His prayer and His mission. If we desire this depth of union, He will never keep us in the dark, never. So constantly we come to Him and draw from Him. He won't get tired of us coming. He is uncreated energy and He desires us to experience Him.

The German theologian, Karl Rahner, tells us that Christians of the future must be mystics or they will not persevere. He's speaking to us, God's little ones. If we are not in this kind of union, the attack can be too great. Our faith can get undermined, and we will fall. Satan is strong, but no one is stronger than God and His love. No one. We are called to be mystics. We are called to know things that God knows, to see things that God sees, and to feel what God feels. We are called to be clothed with this kind of power from on high. We must always remember that the armor we need is the armor of God. We can't go out and purchase it, not even one little piece. It's not for sale. It is gift, and it's given only by God. When the armor hasn't been fully given yet and we're not fully clothed, God in His mercy protects us. He is saying that we're not fully ready yet. We know we're not ready, but when God gives His armor, then it is God who is making the decision that we're ready to use it. He is initiating our growth through this gift. It is He who is preparing us.

Whenever I have gone to Medjugorje, I have spent a great deal of time at the foot of the blue cross. It has a lot of memories and meaning to me, and I find Our Lady there. So at the foot of the blue cross, I was pondering with Mary about the visionaries and the privilege they have of speaking with her every single day and having their prayer life being directed by her. I was thinking, "It would just be wonderful to have you as my spiritual director. I can't imagine what that would be like. It would be wonderful." She spoke, and she was smiling. She said, "Oh, no. I would want you to have the same spiritual director that I had." I said, "What? Who is that?" She said, "The Holy Spirit. He taught me everything I ever knew about love." So I thought, "I'll settle for the Holy Spirit!" This is what

Mary wants for all of us. Mothers want to share everything they have with their children. Mothers have such great big generous giving hearts, and Mary is the Mother of mothers. She wants to share everything she has with us. She wants us to have the same director of our souls that she had: the Holy Spirit Himself. It's so beautiful.

I remember the first time we visited Medjugorje. We had a few prayer requests to give Jelena, one of the interior locutionists. In 1985, there were hardly any Americans or pilgrims there except the Italian Church. I asked Jelena, "Could you take a few prayer requests to Our Lady?" She said, "No. Our Lady has said that for the next two weeks we're not to do any kind of intercession or answer any requests. It's just a time to be with her." I think this is what convinced me more than anything that Jelena was authentic and was really hearing from Our Lady. That's an excellent spiritual director. We are not in ministry all the time. We can't keep giving and giving and giving without a lot of receiving. Our strength comes from the Lord.

We see a lot of burnout in the Church today, and mainly it's because people are not receiving enough. Burnout is seldom caused by doing too much; it's usually caused by not receiving enough. One of the most powerful tools of the enemy and a big temptation today is that we get busy, busy, busy. We are busy about good things. We're giving, we're doing, we're serving, but if we don't take time to balance and to receive from the Lord, then pretty soon we are running on empty, and we will go into burnout. One time I was pondering the names of the Trinity. I said to Mary, "We know the First Person of the Trinity as Father, so we call Him Father. He has a name. The Second Person of the Trinity we call Jesus. Who do you call the Third Person of the Trinity? Does He have a name?" And then she quoted her own Magnificat and said, "His Name is Holy" (Lk 1:49). He is holy and this is our strength. We have to be taken more and more into the holiness of God

Himself, into that unity. This is how we become strengthened. The Holy Spirit is the Sanctifier. He is always at work within us, activating the gifts that He gives us, bringing us more into conformity with God's perfect will. The Holy Spirit is constantly bringing us into deeper union with Jesus and bringing us into the deeper revelation and experience of the Father. There is an inner divine mystery to the triune life cycle that God is sharing with us. It's the very heart of God: God's Spirit, the Holy Spirit. It is the Spirit who is pure Love.

In the Gospel of John, Jesus meets a woman at a well who is in a state of sin. He reveals Himself to her before anyone else has had the revelation of who He really is, not even His own apostles. His Mother obviously knew who He was, I think Joseph knew who He was, but the rest of the people didn't know yet. So Jesus comes to the well and meets this woman. She's had several husbands and the man she's living with now is not even her husband. She comes to the well for a drink because she's thirsty. She comes at noon because she was not really welcomed and accepted by the other women in the town who would be getting their water in the morning. Jesus then reveals who He is to her and starts to teach her. He said, "If only you recognized God's gift" (Jn 4:10). It was as if He was encouraging her, saying, "If you could but experience this kind of love, this other love wouldn't hold its power over you." Jesus was offering her this great gift of Love, the Holy Spirit, because He knew that she was thirsty for Love.

That's all He asks of us: to be thirsty and to be hungry for Love. He wants us to seek, and He will come and reveal that great gift of His. God is love and He wants to communicate with love, through love, and in love. He is a God of the heart. God is looking for lovers, passionate lovers, because that's who He is. This love of the Father, poured forth through the Holy Spirit, is the strength that prayer warriors need. Nothing, nothing can overcome love. Nothing is stronger. Nothing can quench love. Satan knows that so he does everything to keep us from prayer in order to keep us from receiving and drinking deeply of this love.

We need to be careful of what is happening during our prayer. Sometimes people will say, "Something's wrong with my prayer. I don't know what it is. God doesn't hear me. God doesn't love me. God doesn't answer me." I'll say, "Tell me about your prayer. What are you doing? What happened?" "Well, I have a special devotion that I say every day. I have a particular litany I like to recite. I go to Mass. I say the Divine Office. I pray the rosary." It can go on and on! It's all things that *we* are doing. If our prayer is all what we are doing, then our prayer is out of balance. We must give God equal time to do for us. We are the ones who are standing in the need of prayer. We are the poor ones. We are the little ones. Hopefully, we're the empty ones. We have need of Him, not the other way around, and as God fills us, then we will have more to give. We will have love.

Our Lady at Medjugorje said something similar when the question was put, "Sometimes you say we're to pray and be filled with the Lord. Then you say we're also to do the corporal works of mercy, to visit the sick, to visit those in prison. What are we to do?" The answer came back, "We are to do both." It's not an either/or situation. It's not that some are to strictly pray and others only to do active apostolic work. Somehow there's a split in the thinking of the Church. There are the contemplatives in one part of the Church and those in the apostolic ministry in another part, but this is not the spirituality of Jesus. Jesus and Mary are contemplatives. They hear, receive, and drink deeply, but after they have heard, received, and are filled with whatever God has spoken to them, then they do. They receive; then they give.

Scripture tells us that while Jesus was at prayer He was absorbed, spending the night in communion with God (Lk 6:12). This is a beautiful word and a wonderful description of contemplative spirituality. When we are absorbed in something, we are just drinking it in, totally immersed. It is like putting some ink on a blotter or water on a sponge. They just absorb the ink and water. Jesus was like this in the presence of the Father. He was absorbed in the Father, in the full sense of receptivity, of receiving, and look at the fruitfulness of His ministry. He spent the remainder of His days giving away the love He had received in prayer, using that power and love. However, when He Himself was in that kind of prayer, He was not in that action of giving. Rather, He was receiving the Father and the Spirit. He was receptive, and so He was filled.

I often think that we take better care of our cars than we do of ourselves. Who can drive a car on empty? But how many times do we try to go on empty? We need a constant filling of the Holy Spirit. Once again we are talking about experience. An hour can go by in prayer and we think, "My, nothing has happened. Something is wrong here." But the fruit of our prayer is that we are energized and a lot of good things happen throughout the day. That's one of the things about this type of spirituality. We may not think anything is happening because sometimes it's just love. We are just drinking in love.

Have you ever been with someone you love and you don't speak at all? Speaking would almost mar it and besides, there's no need for words. No words are necessary when people are experiencing love. In this kind of experience with God, oftentimes there are no particular thoughts or words. We are just drinking and eating like in the beautiful twenty-third Psalm where the Good Shepherd is leading His sheep. We are His sheep, His flock, and He is leading us to green pastures and still waters. As we go deep within, the waters fill us more and more. This happens in the ocean. As we get deeper into the ocean, we get more and more filled, more and more quiet. The whole storm is on the surface of the ocean but we never would know it. Nothing can disturb the peace of a soul that is sunk into God like that.

Elizabeth of the Trinity knew how to experience this union with the Trinity. Although she died at the age of twenty-six, she had a tremendous devotion to the Trinity and many experiences of the Trinity. She would go into prayer and just sink into her Three. Isn't that beautiful? But for us it takes a little while to just sink. We have to get distractions out of the way, as we are looking to just sink into that deep presence of God within. God has made His home within us. Each of us individually is a house of God. We might say we're like His home away from home. This is where He lives. He's always there, but the one who may not be at home may be ourselves. We may be always preoccupied with other thoughts. We may be busy someplace else mentally. We may be the ones that might not be home, but God is at home. Collectively we are a house of God. We are Church. In the Old and New Testament God said, "My house shall be called a house of prayer" (Lk 19:46; Is 56:7; Mt 21:13; Mk 11:17). He wants each of us individually to be a house of prayer. This means union, communication.

The word prayer is so misused today. There are several different concepts of prayer, so I don't really have a definition of prayer to give you. There are books and books of definitions of prayer. The saints have written eloquently and spoken of prayer already. We have such a heritage of prayer in our Church. We are so rich. We need to remember that prayer is communication of some kind. It does not have to be verbal. It can be communication of presence, but it is a connecting. This is how we look at prayer. Prayer really is nothing more than a telephone, but a telephone is important if we want to call someone we

116

love. Once we hear that voice, once the connection is made, we are not even conscious that we are using the telephone anymore. It is only a means to connect to the other party. This is what prayer really is: it is the connection. Once we have made the connection, we are receiving, we are being loved, we are being strengthened, we are being taught, and we are being healed. All kinds of things are happening because we are in a relationship.

God is interested in relationships. Satan is also interested in relationships, but He wants to destroy relationships among people and families in the Church, in our nation, and in other nations and countries. Satan uses communication for his own purposes so much because God is interested in communication and God speaks to us through our relationship with Him. Everything about God has to do with relationship, not with what He does. We in the Western Church put so much emphasis on what we do. We get so much of our identity from what we do, but this isn't who we are at all. Since we are programmed this way, when we have failures at what we do, we think we are a failure. We are not.

It's a very interesting Scripture where Moses approached the burning bush. The burning bush is very much a symbol of the fire of Love, the Spirit. This is where the strength lies: in that Presence, that Flame. Moses asked God, "If they ask me 'What is his name, what am I to tell them?" (Ex 3:13) God's reply is really extraordinary. God answered, "I am who am" (Ex 3:14). His whole emphasis is on His Person, who He is, not what He does. In other words, "I will be for you who I will be for you." We can't typecast Him, we can't box Him in, we can't put a label on Him. He could have said, "Well, I'm a healer. I'm a deliverer. I'm a creator. I'm a sanctifier." He could have said all the things that He does, but He didn't say any of that. His priority is relationship. This is who I am. While at prayer, we can forget all about ministry. We can forget about doing and everything else, and just be. Just be. It's hard for us to just be. We almost feel guilty sometimes if we're not doing something, anything, even talking to God. We think, "I should be doing something."

We should simply be in the process of becoming: becoming a saint and becoming full of God's love. God is looking for saints. These are His prayer warriors. He doesn't have a lot of friends, real friends, people who are really surrendered to Him and let Him have His way. He's looking for people who will let Him wave the white flag all the time and walk under it. God doesn't have that. We live in a rebellious Church. We live in a very disobedient nation, but the hopeful part is that God works with remnants. God doesn't need numbers. He doesn't need huge crowds, but what He needs are faithful ones. He needs little ones whom He can use *His* way in *His* time. Our Lady prayed, "Be it done unto me." There's no control there but total openness and total receptivity. "Let it be done to me as you say" (Lk 1:38). Your way, Your plan, Your time. It takes a lot of trust, but look at the fruit. Look what happened to Mary. She was full of life, full of love, full of Jesus. This is the kind of prayer and lifestyle that God is calling each and every one of us to today.

There is another very important point here: preparation. Preparation is essential. We have to be full of God's light. It was during the Nazareth days that Jesus was prepared for the confrontations to come. We spend so much time talking about and learning what He said those last three years of His life. It's amazing that when we are going to teach a little child anything, we really don't use words. We don't tell a child how to tie his shoe; we show him.

God looks upon us as children, and He is showing us something extremely important. This man, Jesus, lived only thirty-three years and look where He spent most of his life: thirty years of silence and hiddenness. "Jesus, for His part, progressed steadily in wisdom and age and grace" (Lk

2:52). We know He was wise at the age of twelve, having already taught in the temple. We don't see Him again until He's about thirty years old. Look at what God is showing us. Somehow we have missed the importance of the Nazareth days, the importance of the hidden life. He loved the hidden life. He's hidden within us. The Spirit is so hidden that we can't see Him. We know His movement because we can see, "Oh that must have been the Spirit. I just had this thought. It wasn't mine." Or we see the fruit from an action, and we know it was the Spirit. His activity within us is so hidden.

Jesus wants us to be comfortable with the hiddenness of His life continuing within us now. In this silence we learn to discern the voice of God. It is in the silence that we really learn who He is. We experience Him, we know Him, so that even when satan comes, disguises, and counterfeits God's voice, we will know it's not authentic. We will be able to shut it right off. Jesus said, "When you pray, go to your room" (Mt 6:6). Those who go deep into that inner room will know that voice. We will know God's voice whether it comes over TV or through a child, whether His words come through prayer or through a friend, we will know it. Once we know His voice we will be able to shut out all other voices. We will know His voice and that's the voice we will follow. "The sheep follow him because they recognize his voice" (Jn 10:4). We, too, shall follow because we know His voice.

We have sheep at Bellwether, and we have learned an immense amount of things from these sheep. The brother who has fed them and raised them from birth is the only one they will follow. No matter how good we are to them, they will not follow us. So if we can't get the sheep in, we have to go get this brother to get the sheep in. They won't listen to us. I said, "Lord I see what You are saying. You are showing us that Your sheep know You." God is so good. God is so good! We have to be comfortable in the silence, and **"Draw our strength from the Lord and from His mighty power"** (Eph 6:10).

Chapter 7

The Sword of the Spirit

"Take . . . the sword of the Spirit,
the word of God."
Eph 6:17

There is a lot of mystery to be found in the sword of the Spirit, which is the Word of God. We will never exhaust the depth of the mystery. There will always be more to learn. When we think of the Word of God, we are thinking primarily of the Second Person of the Trinity, Jesus. "In the beginning was the Word; the Word was in God's presence, and the Word was God. He was present to God in the beginning" (Jn 1:1-2). So before He became Jesus, He was the Word of God. When the Word became flesh and took on our humanity, He became Jesus. I pondered this a lot and could never quite fully understand it, and I still don't fully understand it, but what I hear is that the Sword which the Spirit uses *is* Jesus. The Holy Spirit uses Jesus as His weapon. He is the Weapon of all weapons.

We need the strength of God and the power of the Spirit, but we need the sword of the Spirit to actually do the fighting, the combat itself. This sword that the Holy Spirit uses is Jesus, the Word of God Himself. No wonder we are empowered! The Spirit uses the Word of God, enfleshed now in us, to fight this battle. No wonder He needs us. No wonder He's counting on us. He seeks to use the Jesus deep within us as this sword. If we are in union with Jesus, we have become the sword of the Spirit. There is a lot to ponder!

There are many ways that we receive the Word. We have the Word as the written word in Scripture, but it's not a living Word unless the Holy Spirit overshadows it and gives it power. Otherwise, I can read the Bible like any other book but it won't be living. It must take root in me and become flesh of my flesh and bone of my bone to become anointed and empowered by the Spirit. Then it will become alive and dynamic and, hopefully, effective!

When we begin our prayer with Scripture, we need to always ask for the overshadowing of the Holy Spirit. We ask the Spirit to come upon whatever He really wants us to understand, what He wants us to know, and what He wants us to receive. We are changing and growing all the time, so each time we ponder or meditate on the Word, even if it's that same verse, it will be different because the Spirit comes upon it. We will be receiving truth at a different level each time. There will be different circumstances in our lives now than when we read it before, and it will be exactly what we need to hear. Through this anointing, this light that comes, we will know what to do because the Spirit has directed us and has used His Word, His Living Word to speak to us.

"As for you, the anointing you received from him remains in your hearts. This means you have no need for anyone to teach you. Rather, as his anointing teaches you about all things and is true, free from any lie, remain in him as that anointing taught you" (1 Jn 2:27). This is a powerful Scripture that I encourage you to really meditate and ponder it with Our Lady and take it to heart. We are being led and taught by God through the contemplative John. "His anointing is true, free from any lie" (1 Jn 2:27). It is so rare when we can receive a teaching or a truth today that is free from any kind of deception. So this deep relationship and union with the Spirit and the Living Word is so important.

One beautiful thing about the Holy Trinity is that just when we are becoming interested in one Person of the Trinity, that Person will direct us to another member of the Trinity. I don't know if you've had this experience in your own prayer life. We have a personal relationship with Jesus, and He teaches us to go to the Father. He taught us to pray to the Father, not to Himself. So we do that, and then what happens? We get to the mountaintop, we get into union with the Father, and what does He say on Mount Tabor? "This is my Son, my beloved. Listen to Him" (Mk 9:6). Once we draw near to one Person of the Trinity, that Person will introduce us to a newer, deeper relationship with another Person of the Trinity. The Father, Son, and Spirit are one, and they are constantly drawing us into this oneness with them.

This is making the very strong assumption that we are listening, and we know what He is telling us. I think the main problem in the Church today for the people who are really trying to follow the Lord is not disobedience, even though it looks like there is a lot of disobedience. I think the deeper problem is that people are just not listening to God. They are not taking the time to listen and are not going into the quietness so they don't hear from the Lord. The discipline needed to listen and to wait upon the Lord has not been developed. So I think a great majority of Christians today have no idea of what God is saying. They may not be doing "Whatever He tells you" (Jn 2:5) because they may have no idea He's even speaking to them. This is one of the big complaints of the Lord all throughout the Bible, particularly in the Old Testament, over and over and over. "If only my people would hear me, and walk in my ways" (Ps 81:14).

It's like God can't get our attention because it's not always a priority for us to listen. Children sometimes have a difficult time listening, and we do, too. There are many things that block our listening. Again, the enemy is very active in this area because it has to do with communication, particularly communication that will lead us into union with the Trinity. This kind of union with the Word, with Jesus, will change us. This is called transforming union. We're talking here about changing so much that we become the Word. Transforming union allows the Word to be so fully enfleshed within us that we become extensions, you might say, of His Incarnation. Jesus can live once again but this time within us. He will transform us slowly, step by step, as a growth process that He chooses to go through within us. When we are baptized, we are in the infancy stage spiritually so we have to allow for the Nazareth days. We have to allow time for our growth spiritually.

One time when I was praying in the cloister I made a statement, and after I made it I felt foolish. Love does many foolish things. We do things out of love before we process them, and this is just what I did. I realized it was really a ridiculous thing to say to God after I said it. I asked Him, "Is there anything I have that You need?" Here I am with vows of every kind imaginable, living in total poverty, spiritually as well as physically, and yet I am thinking that I might have something He needs. As I look back, I realize it was probably the Holy Spirit prompting me to ask the question. I was amazed when right from the Tabernacle Jesus said, "Yes." I said, "Really, what is it?" "Your body. I need your body."

Now that should be obvious to us: if He's going to become enfleshed again, He needs us. As we pray, we're beginning to see more and more what God wants us to know about the armor. He wants to show us how to wear it and how to use it. It's a need that God has to use His Jesus fully alive now within us. He needs us for His war. He needs us for His confrontation. He needs us for the Church. He needs us for His greater honor and glory. This is amazing.

As a convert, I was raised with the Baltimore Catechism, and I remember that it said that God created us out of nothing. That always kind of bothered me, but when I came to prayer, I brought that nothing kind of attitude with me. One day the Lord challenged me about this attitude. I said, "Well, didn't You create me out of nothing?" He said, "No, I created you out of love." He creates us out of love. In His love for souls, His love for mankind's salvation, and His great desire for all of us to spend eternity with Him, He still continues to work through love, the love of His Spirit, the love of His Son. We will never fully understand this tremendous love of the Trinity for us in this life, only in the next. We occasionally get little glimpses of how they work in unison. The Trinity works together, Father, Son, and Spirit, one God. They work together.

We have such a tremendous devotion to the Trinity. There are so many stories in the Bible where God has shown us that He moves in union with the Son and the Spirit. "Let us make man in our image, after our likeness" (Gn 1:26). I remember the first time I prayed that, I thought, "Let *us*." We always think of God as Yahweh. The people of the Old Testament didn't know about the Trinity, yet Scripture remains, "Let *us*" and "*Our* image." It's so beautiful that we are made in the image and likeness of the Trinity. This is tremendous! So right there, it made me wonder, "What are You really like? Who are You? If I'm made in Your image and in Your likeness, then the only way I'm going to know who I really am and who I am really like is to know more about You because I am a reflection of You." This is a springboard for more mystery, for a walk into another area of His love.

Another instance where the Trinity moves in unison is at the Annunciation. Our Lady received a revelation of the Trinity, and she questioned, "How can this be since I do not know man?" (Lk 1:34) Gabriel answered, "The Holy Spirit will come upon you (that's the Third Person of the Trinity) and the power of the Most High (that's their Yahweh, God, the First Person, the Most High) will overshadow you; hence, the holy offspring to be born will be called the Son of God" (Lk 1:35). There it is, the Trinity being revealed to Mary. I wonder how much she understood. She wouldn't have known anything without this revelation, this light. It's so beautiful.

There are so many ways that we see the Trinity working. In John 14:6, Jesus Himself said, "I am the way (the Second Person of the Trinity) and the truth (the Third Person, the Spirit) and the life" (the Father). We see that Jesus always moved in total concert with the Trinity over and over again in His teachings. They move as one. They are one God. We see it on Calvary; the Trinity is there. The Trinity is very present in the Scripture of the woman at the well. "If only you recognized God's gift" (Jn 4:10). Jesus is referring to the Spirit in the life-giving water. "The Father seeks those who worship him in Spirit and in truth" (Jn 4:23-24). It's beautiful the way Scripture comes alive and starts to feed us. We start to receive food, spiritual food, knowledge, and wisdom, and our relationship with the Trinity starts to blossom.

The gifts of the Holy Spirit become activated through the Word, Jesus. We become stronger, start to grow, and Scripture becomes alive. This happens very much in silence. Silence is so important in developing this union, but it is difficult to find in our world today. But it is in this silence that God can speak to us. When God is going to move in power, in tremendous gift, in tremendous revelation, He moves in the atmosphere of silence.

So we need to look at our days. What kind of time and space have we carved out to develop and nurture that silence so we can listen to the Father? In order for the gift of revelation to flow, we must provide this atmosphere of silence. All contemplative spirituality is gift, God's gift to us of sharing His mind, sharing His Heart, sharing His Word, and sharing His Life with us. He wants to give us these deeper gifts, and He does it in the silence in a special way. Not that He can't do it at other times because He does, but special revelation can happen in the silence.

For example, look at what happened to this woman filled full of grace at the Annunciation. In the silence of her heart united to the Father, tremendous mystery and revelation could be received by Mary. Tremendous revelation took place at the Resurrection. Who was there? Look even at Bethlehem. We don't know for sure if anyone other than Mary and Joseph were there at the actual birthing, but apparently not.

There are many Scriptures encouraging us to come into this silence. "Silence in the presence of the Lord God! for near is the day of the Lord" (Zep 1:7). We need to come into this deeper silence because God is getting ready to move in a sovereign way. John the contemplative alludes to this sovereign movement of God as the seals are in the process of being opened. "When the Lamb broke open the seventh seal, there was silence in heaven for about half an hour" (Rv 8:1). This is going to be probably the greatest movement of God that we will ever see, and it's coming very soon: when there is silence in heaven, the choirs of angels in heaven are silent, and all the praying is silent. This is tremendous mystery. I urge each of you to go into the silence and receive the revelation that the Lord wants to share with you. God loves the silence.

"Be still and know that I am God" (Ps 46:10 or 11). Again, that word *know*, "Know that I am God." It is in this kind of stillness and silence that we have the experience of God. Our God so desires to speak to us and to have us know Him. "I will lure her," her being the Church, "I will lure her into the desert and there I will speak to her heart" (Hos 2:16). We also see the desire of God's heart that we come to know Him in Revelation 12. We see the reference to the Woman being Our Lady, but the Woman also being prototype of the

127

Church. God wants to give the gift of contemplative spirituality again to His Church. Contemplative spirituality has always been in the Church, but it's going to come in a fuller way now because the Church is being called to come into the desert, into the silence, into this other level of prayer. We are being called into the silence to hear God, to know Him, and to experience Him. God is trying to prepare us, the Church. The Church has always been prepared in the desert and has always been renewed through desert spirituality. These desert experiences are nothing to be afraid of for they will bring strength and vitality to the Church through this union with the Trinity. This is what God is trying to do now.

Jesus wants His Church to hear His words. He wants His Church to once again become a prophetic Church, a Church that teaches His Word, a Church that speaks His Word, lives His Word, and witnesses to His Word. In Ezekiel 37:4 we read, "Then He said to me, `Prophesy over these bones, and say to them: Dry bones, hear the word of the Lord!' " The contemplative John said "What we have seen and heard we proclaim in turn to you" (1 Jn 1:3). This is witnessing first hand, not recounting what we read about. People know when we know the Lord. They can feel the fire and love from deep within us. It just pours out and they receive. Have you ever met somebody who really impressed you and then, like the woman at the well, you run and tell everybody. They know because we're excited, we have had a first hand experience, and this vibrancy rubs off on others.

When I was in Medjugorje in the very early days, no one had even heard of Fr. Jozo, he had a little church a few miles away. He was teaching so I went with a group of pilgrims. Fr. Jozo was teaching in German to the German Church that was there. I couldn't understand a word he said, but I thought, "Oh my goodness. I've seen the Lord." What did I do? I went back to Medjugorje and told our group, "You've got to come over to this little town and see and hear this priest. "Well, what did he say?" "Well, I don't know, but it's the Lord." That's witnessing, isn't it? This is what God wants today.

God wants us to have the experience of Him so that we know what He's like. He wants us to have the experience of Him so we understand what He is saying. Once we know Him, then we're going to tell others. When we really find something that's beautiful and special, we want to share it, we want to tell. We'll tell the whole world. Evangelization will be easy! Right now evangelization is very difficult, particularly for Catholics. Maybe it's because we don't have the experience of the Good News to share.

There are two things about Good News that goes far beyond the Bible. First of all, is it new? Are there new things happening in our prayer or are we still living out of an experience from last year or from when we were a child? Is it new? It is like picking up a Sunday paper on Wednesday. It's kind of stale; it's old news. Second of all, it is also *good* news. Jesus said, "No one is good but God alone" (Lk 18:19). So we're talking about something that comes from God: it's new, it's good, and we're excited about it.

We should be receiving this good news in our prayer. Some people call it "ramah." It's a word, a concept, or a truth that we learn each day that we can hold onto throughout that day. We may not understand it fully, we may not be able to share it right at that moment. Sometimes we share the fruit of our prayer before it's ripened, before we have received all of the good news that God has for us, all of the maturity, all of the teaching. If we pick it and share it too soon, we lose it ourselves. It didn't grow into maturity. We have to be careful when to share and when not to share. We need to let the fruit from our prayer grow until we begin to understand it. We need to wait until it becomes so firmly rooted within us that we can taste it. "Taste and see how good the Lord is" (Ps 34:9).

This ramah might be something that happened in the Scripture or something we heard at Mass. Maybe we don't have time to ponder that word or something the priest said in his homily right then. We can keep a little pocket notebook with us and write that word down where there was that quickening in our spirit, something our heart heard to ponder later. We must become very sensitive to the movement of the Spirit in our hearts. Then later when we have time in our prayer period, bring it before the Lord and ask, "You were overshadowing this particular word for me today. What is it? What is it now that You want me to know and learn from it?"

At Bellwether, we have shared reflections every day. It's fascinating because something happens when we hear the Word that doesn't happen when we read it. Even in your private prayer, feel free to read Scripture out loud and hear it yourself. By the time we celebrate Mass, most of us have already had prayer periods and time with the Lord in silence and solitude. Everyone has already read the Scripture of the day and maybe had a whole beautiful meditation on it. But when the Word is read at Mass, everybody hears something different that they didn't hear at all in their morning meditations. We hear it right then. We don't know the whole teaching of it, but it is giving us life. That's what I mean when I say something is anointed. It is being overshadowed by the Spirit. He is, as we say in the Creed every Sunday, "the Lord and giver of Life." Let Him give Life to His Word because we need to be fed. We need to be fed with the Body and Blood of Jesus. We also need to be fed with the Word.

One time when I was still in the cloister, praying in the chapel alone, the Lord said, "Just watch the sisters come in. Just watch." As they were coming for the next prayer session, I was watching them and watching them genuflect. After awhile, I said, "Well, what is it that I'm supposed to be seeing here?" He said, "Did you notice the ones who are

130

really aware that I am here and the ones who are not?" We can tell whether someone is aware of His Presence even by the way they genuflect. The Lord showed me that even though He is there in the Tabernacle, there in His real Presence, He is not present to everyone who comes into the church. It's our awareness that brings Him into us. So just going to Mass and doing certain rituals without acknowledging the true Presence of Jesus may not help us grow in our faith. Jesus is really present there in His Body and Blood, and He can be more and more present as we allow His Presence to happen within us.

For example, we can think of a loved one who is someplace else, and just by that thought, that awareness, we can bring them to us because we carry them in our hearts, we carry them in our minds, we carry them in our lives. On the other hand, we may have sat in the same room with someone and not been present to them because we are someplace else in our thoughts, or they're not present to us because they're somewhere else. The mind and the discipline of the mind have a great deal to do with prayer and our awareness of the presence of the Lord. There are disciplines in prayer. Even prayer is an art. There is something we always have to learn, and it is God who will teach us. It always has to do with love.

When I entered the cloister, I was never taught any methods of prayer. They never taught us about the ways the saints prayed. All they talked about was Jesus. I began to see the dynamic of novitiate training: as we began to fall more and more in love with Jesus, it became easier for us to pray because we wanted to be with Him. We wanted to be with the Person whom we loved. We wanted to be in some sort of communication with Him at all times. We never wanted to be apart. It's so simple, but if we find that this desire to be in constant relationship with Jesus doesn't happen, then we need to simply ask for that desire. If we desire this union, it will happen. If we begin to get hungry and thirsty, it will happen. We will seek out the food. We will seek out the drink. But if we are so full of ourselves, rich in our own gifts and our own little lifestyles, then there is no need for relationship.

This is why the little ones, the poor ones, and the empty ones are so important to God. We need Him, and we know it. He comes then to meet our need and that's what He loves to do more than anything. One time I said to Him, "I've just begun to realize that You deliberately made us weak, limited, and imperfect." I went through the whole litany of all these weaknesses in myself and said, "You could supply everything but You did not want to be left out of anything we think, say, or do." It was like He said, "That's right. You've finally come to understand. You cannot do anything without Me."

So let the Word, Jesus, become enfleshed within you and grow. Do not stifle the Spirit. Do not stifle Scripture. Let them speak to you. Let Jesus communicate again with His Father through you. He loves to do that. He will share with us what He is communicating. Let Jesus continue to surrender and be led by the Spirit because He wants to live His life again in each of us. There really isn't room in these little temples of ours for two. One time He told me, "One of us has to go." And He said, "Guess who it's going to be!" So let Him live. We will find love. We will find joy, peace, and happiness. We will find ourselves, our true selves because we will find God.

It's very important to journal. By my nature, I do not like to journal. I'm of a temperament where I like to dream. I'm the dreamer, so I have to discipline myself to write things down, especially the things spoken to my heart. I have found that I pay a great price if I don't. We can't remember from day to day those little manifestations of God's love, and when those desert days come when we can't quite find the oasis, satan will come in those barren times and our thought life can disintegrate. "God never speaks to me. He never answers my prayer. He never shows me anything." We can forget so easily. It's not because we are forgetful. Somehow it seems like we never forget the hurts, the negatives, or what people have done to us. But we so easily forget what God has done for us day after day after day. So it's good to jot down some notes so we can go back and review them during those dry times. "Oh, yes. I forgot that He showed me that last Wednesday. Oh, Lord, thank You. I did ask You that and You did do something about it." It's what we call Prayer of Recollection. We re-collect all these wonderful things He's done. This carries us over many of the dry times so we don't feel discouraged, we don't feel abandoned, and satan doesn't get in there.

There are many different ways to journal. One of the ways we journal is the love letter type. We usually write a little note to the Lord about something, Scripture, anything that seems important. It's usually something that we don't understand or something we want to know more about. It can be something that doesn't even have to do with Scripture like, "Lord, what are You thinking about right now? What are You doing? You live within me. What do you do all day?" Have you ever thought about that? He has some beautiful things to say about that, too, but let Him respond to you in your writing. Whatever you write, whether "Dear Jesus," "Dear Father," or "Dear Holy Spirit," allow the Lord to respond. The first sentence might be us; it probably will be us. For example, He might say, "My very dear friend," but it probably won't be until about the second sentence that we'll begin to get inspired. We need to let go of the control and gently allow ourselves to begin to get inspired. We will see so much goodness come forth. Wisdom will start taking over within, and we will begin to learn and see many things.

We know Scripture tells us we are made in the image and likeness of God (Gn 1:27), but we don't really have a deep grasp of God, who He really is and what He's really like.

We don't always know who we really are and what we're like. We need to know who we are. Our identity is extremely important. If we don't know this, satan will really play havoc with us, and the lies about ourselves will come. Our identity must be firmly rooted in the Trinity. One of the ways to encourage this is to begin asking the question Jesus asked Peter and His apostles, "Who do you say that I am?" (Mt 16:15; Mk 8:29; Lk 9:20) The apostles each had different answers, but it was Peter who had the right answer. Only Peter had the right answer because he had had the revelation now from God the Father. He said, "You are the Messiah, the Son of the living God" (Mt 16:16). Jesus replied, "No mere man has revealed this to you but my heavenly Father" (Mt 16:17).

This is what I'm talking about. Flesh and blood has told us so many times who we are, and so many times it has been mistaken. Parents might have said, "You're stupid. You don't know anything. Why don't you grow up?" Many of us have a lot of that going on within us, and it has damaged our identity. Schoolteachers may have damaged our identity. Many wives take their identity from their husbands, but that's not the image any of us are made in. We're not even made in the image of our parents. We are made in the image and likeness of God (Gn 1:27). So we need to go to God and ask, "Who do You say that I am? I know who my mom says, who my dad says, who my friends say, but Father, who do You say I am?" We can have a lot of identities and can be a divided house, but we're a house of God. A house divided against itself will fall (Lk 11:17).

Prayer warriors have to know who they are in God's sight. So keep asking these questions in your prayer time. Start with the Person of the Trinity who you are most comfortable with. If you feel most comfortable with Jesus, then ask Him, "Jesus, who do You say that I am?" This is very important to know because our relationship is in our identity. Mary's identity to the Trinity gave her different roles. In her relationship with the Father, she's daughter. In her relationship with Jesus, she's Mother. In her relationship with the Spirit, she's spouse. In a family, the mother has a different relationship with the children than she has with her husband. How the children are going to answer this question will be different from how her husband answers.

So when the Father responds to our question of who we are, He is going to let us know who we are in relationship to Him. Jesus will let us know our true identity in relationship to Him, and the Holy Spirit will let us know who we truly are in our relationship with Him. Then we are going to get a wonderful concept of who we really are: made in the image and likeness of God. Once we believe and know that we are truly made in the image and likeness of God, nothing can come against this. Satan will never get that victory over us. We will have that knowledge of who we really are, and what a mighty weapon this is!

"Take . . . the sword of the Spirit, the word of God" (Eph 6:17). He is enfleshed in each one of us to the degree to which we allow Him to change us into His image and likeness. May the Father, Son and Holy Spirit find a dwelling place deep within us.

Chapter 8

Pray in the Spirit

"At every opportunity, pray in the Spirit,
using prayers and petitions of every sort.
Pray constantly and attentively
for all in the holy company."
Eph 6:18

We are seeking the heart and mind and wisdom of God. This will be our protection. As we continue further in Ephesians 6, examining our armor and weapons, Paul continues to teach us, "At every opportunity pray in the Spirit" (Eph 6:18). He is encouraging us to pray constantly, in fact to pray without ceasing (1 Thes 5:17). I used to wonder, "How can that be done? We have to sleep. There are other things to do." But as we come more and more into union with the Word, who is the Intercessor, who is the Prayer, the Prayer Warrior, we will find that He takes over. He is the One who is praying without ceasing. He is the One who is praying always. He prays even when we're sleeping because our heart is always awake, and God lives so much in the heart! So it's wonderful! It **can** be done. Prayer was Mary's lifestyle, and we are called to that same lifestyle. We are to allow the Lord to completely take over our lives and to pray without ceasing within us.

This part of the armor focuses on prayer and praying in the Holy Spirit, with the Holy Spirit, and led by the Holy Spirit. We have found that the way to use the sword, the Word of God, Jesus, effectively is to allow the Spirit to lead us. Jesus, the Word of God, is the sword of the Spirit. The way we use the sword is through prayer. Why? Because Paul tells us that Jesus now has obtained a far more excellent ministry, that of intercession. Isn't that amazing? Of all the things Jesus did, Paul says that now He has obtained a far more excellent ministry, that of intercession (Heb 8:6). This ministry of intercession takes place at the right hand of the Father, who is on His throne in heaven.

As we go back to the woman and the dragon scene, we read that right after she gave birth to a Son, her child was caught up to God and to His throne (Rv 12:5). Jesus is on His throne in a very special way: He is King, He's King of kings and Lord of lords. He is the Lamb who is risen, and He is in power. Jesus at the Father's right hand is now in this tremendous powerful ministry of intercessory prayer. He is able to do this ministry again by taking up residency in human beings, in flesh and blood like us. So Jesus, in that incarnate spirituality, can intercede again through us, with us, and in us, all for the greater honor and glory of the Father. It's the beautiful cycle of God's love. God could have set it up otherwise where He would intervene directly whenever we needed it. However, in God's great love for us, He decided to allow us to be part of His work. Jesus is **the** Intercessor, and God will not move without intercession. We may wonder how much more would be accomplished in the world today if there were more intercessors allowing Jesus to continue His powerful ministry with, in, and through them.

Jesus has told us over and over again to *ask*. He stressed so much the need to ask, knowing that He wanted this ministry to continue within us. He said, "Whatever you ask in my name I will do" (Jn 14:13). That's very generous and quite risky; ask anything and I'll do it. Ask anything in My

137

name. When we speak about praying in Jesus' name, we are not talking about pulling a name out of a hat and saying, "In the name of ..." That is not where the power is. The power comes when Jesus is in union with us, and we are in union with Jesus. It's the person who has the name, in this case Jesus, who has the power. When a woman marries, it's because of the marriage, it's because of that union that she takes on the name of her husband and has a right to whatever he has, including his checkbook! That's what we're interested in with the Lord—His checkbook! We can purchase souls with Jesus. Jesus continues His tremendous redemptive ministry through us right now. Paul talks about these graces that Jesus has already won; he said the graces are being distributed through people like us. The graces need to be distributed. This is what intercessors do: we allow the graces of the Redemption to be distributed and channeled through us. Jesus' love can be strong in our emptiness through our constant, "Yes, Lord." This builds up the Church. Now we see the graces flowing in the renewal in the Church, all for the greater honor and glory of God.

We find that we have to begin looking at things a little bit differently, particularly more from God's point of view. St. Paul tells us, "Since you have been raised up in company with Christ, set your heart on what pertains to higher realms where Christ is seated at God's right hand" (Col 3:1). We know what He is doing at God's right hand: He is interceding through us.

Paul continues to encourage us on this journey, "Be intent on things above rather than on things of earth. After all, you have died and your life is hidden now with Christ in God" (Col 3:2-3). Our lives are starting to slowly disappear as we exchange our preferences for Jesus' preferences. We are slowly becoming more and more hidden in Christ. Hopefully we *have* died, and if we haven't given the Lord complete control of our lives, hopefully we're getting closer. We need to allow this dying to ourselves and our preferences so that there can be that mystical death and rising within each of us where Jesus once again is here. It can be a painful experience, but we all want to have this union. We want to know more and more of the power of the Resurrection. We want to become so much like Jesus that when we are praying, the Father hears His Son praying. This is our inheritance, this is our calling, this is our ministry so that we can enter into this mystery and have access with Jesus, in Jesus, and through Jesus to the throne. Then we can ask the Father. This is where intercession receives power.

The great prophet Isaiah says, "Shake off the dust, ascend to the throne, Jerusalem" (Is 52:2). Shake off the dust. Anything that is impure, anything that is holding you earthbound, shake it off and ascend! Let your spirit come forward now to become the thoughts and plans and vision of God. Let your spirit come forward to minister to the Church. The best thing intercessors can do is to get very, very vertical and stay vertical as much as possible. We need that deep relationship with the Father. The effectiveness of our prayers depends on this relationship. This is why we stress relationship: it's absolutely key, it's essential. There is no power apart from the power of God. He's our source, He's our supply, He's our strength.

In the book of Esther, particularly chapter 6, we see that Esther is queen because of her relationship with the king. She has a relationship, she has a position, and because of this relationship, she has access to the king. She can ask for things and get results because of this relationship. Because of that relationship, her intercession saved her entire nation. Wouldn't it be wonderful if our relationship with the King and with Mary, the Queen of Heaven, could be as effective for our nation as Queen Esther's relationship with the king was for hers? America needs our help! The world needs our help!

One time I asked the Lord, "Are You going to let America go under?" He said, "No, but I will bring her to her knees because I love her." So He's going to spank, but He loves us! He loves America, so He's looking for intercessors who have a love for this nation and for our people, and He's asking them to intercede. He needs intercessors to beg Him to spare our nation and our people. He wants to grant these graces that are so desperately needed today to set America free, but He's waiting for us to ask. He's waiting. He wants to work through us to deliver America from the bondage. This terrible slavery of today is far worse than in the time of Abraham Lincoln. He wants to set America free from the sin that has captured her and keeps her now in such terrible captivity.

So let's learn from Esther. She passed through all the portals and roadblocks until she stood face to face with the king. Because of our union with Jesus, we can pass right through the different levels, too, and speak to the Father. We can pass through and go right into the throne room, right to the Father to ask, "Father, deliver us." We have this access only because of our relationship. Isn't that beautiful?

We see the Word of God, the sword of the Spirit, taking up residency within us in this ministry of intercession. This is what He does best. As we pray the prayers, Jesus Himself is asking the Father through us. It's not so much us going before the Father, but rather it is Jesus who is praying. As we allow Jesus to take over more and more of who we are, then when we go before the Father, we take Jesus there. He needs our mouth, our lips, our heart, our yes, and our will to be present here. God will never invade our free will, so He needs us to pray the prayers. He needs our bodies, He needs us to do it.

One time I was meditating on Jesus riding into Jerusalem on the little white donkey. The focus of my whole prayer was on the little donkey. It was so sensitive to the touch of Jesus. God was showing me that He wants us to be these little beasts of burden and carry Him into the city now. He even wants us to carry Him to the Cross now. He wants to continue His redemption through us. Souls that are pure, souls that are obedient, souls that will carry Him wherever He wants to go can continue His mission. Once we carry Him within ourselves, His mission of giving greater honor and glory to His Father can continue.

We learn a lot from the Lord who dwells within; we learn a lot through our prayer. We also learn from the teachings of the Church and the writings of the saints. But we can also learn a lot of strategy from the Bible. We learn God's strategy and we learn satan's. In spiritual warfare, the strategy changes each time. God doesn't let us get into any set patterns. Just because we pray and He does it one way one time, we can't count on praying in this particular manner all the time. There are no set formulas.

For instance, Joshua crossed the Jordan to retake the Promised Land. He captured city after city, town after town. He received new instructions from the Lord on what to do each time, and it was something different for each city. Jericho is the city that we are probably most familiar with. The Lord gave Joshua very specific instructions on how to recapture Jericho. They were to march around Jericho seven times, and then they were to blow their horns. It was easy; it was really fun. Spiritual warfare has its moments of fun and joy! So they marched around the city seven times and blew their horns, and as they celebrated, the walls came tumbling down!

We used to hear a lot about our Protestant friends doing Jericho marches, but the Lord had never spoken to us about doing anything like that so we never did. Then last year during our core group's weekly prayer time, we asked the Lord if He wanted to show us anything, and one day He did. He said that He would like us to start doing some Jericho Marches. So right away we thought, "Oh, yes. We'll pray for this church and that church." We were thinking of all the ways *we* were going to do it and where *we* were going to go. We never quite learn! He is always teaching us! "No, you'll go to where *I* want you to go." He gave us the names of seven churches here in Omaha. We were going to do the whole city! Some of the parishes He wanted us to pray for we would not have thought of.

So we rented a huge Greyhound bus and with all our lay community with us, the bus was packed. I don't know what the bus driver thought; we tried to kind of explain it but . . .! So we started off with the guitars going, the songs going, and the praise going. As we got closer to our destination, word knowledge started coming. The Lord was giving us very specific directions on how to pray. The bus was so huge it had to circle way out and around because it couldn't get into the little, narrow streets. So as we were praying, we really circled the whole parish and a lot of other places besides. We went around and around seven times, just like the Lord instructed us. Then on the seventh time round, we did the festal shout! We had all these little New Year's horns and little hats and tambourines and drums! We could have been heard clear across the city! It was wonderful! Nobody knew we were doing this. In fact, this is the first time I've even mentioned it publicly. Some wonderful, wonderful fruit has come from it. Some of the fruit we saw then and experienced ourselves.

But each of the parishes the Lord led us to was different. There were different problems in each parish, different situations, and therefore different ways to pray. The Lord would spell out for each particular parish exactly how He wanted us to pray. It was really very wonderful. We did one parish a week, so it took us seven weeks.

This Jericho March was one way, one strategy to bring down satan's stronghold (Jos 6). There are many other strategies in the Bible of how God reclaimed His own land. For example, one of the beautiful ways the Lord teaches us is to point out the strategy of the enemy. Sports teams are always studying the strategy of other teams because they want to win the game. We also need to know the enemy and his strategy as well. We don't want to be caught off guard. We don't want to focus on him, but it's always good to know how the enemy works. That's why we spend time learning satan's strategy and his tools.

In the book of Judith, we see that Judith is quite a prayer warrior. There are intercessors, and then there are intercessor-prayer warriors. Judith is quite a prayer warrior! In chapter seven of the book of Judith, we see that up until this time, the enemy was taking town after town after town easily and winning. Now all of a sudden, we come to the place where the Israelites are, and the word came to Holofernes, "Sir, listen to what we have to say that there may be no losses among your troops. These Israelites do not rely on their spears but on the height of the mountains where they dwell. It is not easy to reach the summit of their mountains." They're referring to the Christians who are praying, the eagles, the contemplatives. "Therefore, sir, do not attack them in regular formation lest not a single one of your troops should fall. Stay in your camp and spare all your soldiers" (Jdt 7:11-12). Here is the strategy: they are going to take the Israelites, who live on the mountaintops, in a different way. "Have some of your servants keep control of the source of water that flows out at the base of the mountain for that is where the inhabitants get their water. Then thirst will begin to carry them off and they will surrender their city. Their wives and children will languish with hunger" (Jdt 7:9).

This is exactly the strategy that we are seeing satan using today in the New Age movement. It's really just that simple. The attack is coming in the water supply. The only water supply of Christians is the Holy Spirit. He is the Living Water, and we receive Him daily if we thirst, if we go to the well of salvation and drink. We drink when we receive Him in prayer and through the Sacraments. He alone is the Lord and giver of life. Now the counterfeit has come with another water supply. It's a false thirst, it's a false contemplation, it's a false mysticism. So those drinking from this tainted water can sit for hours in whatever they want to call it. They can contemplate, they can gaze, but they will die of thirst because it is not the waters of God. It is not the living waters. We are seeing this today, and it's very, very frightening. Satan is attacking people who pray through their prayer.

Counterfeit prayer is not easy to spot as the deception is very clever, particularly contemplative spirituality, because contemplatives drink deeply from within. So this false mysticism is turning people within, to go within to drink, but they're not drinking of the Living Water. They think it's prayer, but satan has affected the water supply as in the book of Judith.

I'm sure there are many reasons why this is happening, but one of the reasons that satan got in through false mysticism is because we are made in God's image. We are made to be mystics. We are empty without this deep union with God. We are made to enter into this great mystery of love, to be beyond where we are. We were created to be one with our God. That's our destiny. But the Church has not been teaching this mysticism. The Church has not been teaching prayer. All the saints are mystics. This deep level of union with God is one of our great inheritances here in the Catholic Church, but we're not being taught how to achieve this.

So our people are hungry and thirsty and they turn to false mysticism. They turn to Buddha, they turn to psychology, and they turn to all the programs that we have now. There's nothing wrong with self-help programs unless we are making them the end rather than the means. AA is a wonderful program, but the "higher power" has a name. Right? Let's go beyond to the Spirit. The deception here has so many faces it is tremendous, and this basically is the strategy of the enemy. This is where we have to stop him. This is where our prayer begins, "Lord give people the true Living Water, a new Baptism of the Holy Spirit." We need this!

144

Interestingly, Pope Paul VI wrote about this in his encyclical, *Evangelization in the Modern World.* He said our people need to be re-baptized, not with the sacrament, but with the Spirit. This is unbelievable! Pope Paul VI spelled out the remedy for the current crisis in the Church back in 1975. This encyclical focuses on evangelization. This re-birth is essential if we're going to be effective evangelizers. Pope Paul VI said, "There can be no effective evangelization unless mankind first be regenerated by the power of the Spirit and renewed from within." He said we need the Baptism of the Holy Spirit.

We need to get the message out and let people know that there *is* another level of union, that their hunger and thirst are authentic, but the way that they are seeking it is not. We need to remove the falsehood, the deception, the blindness, and the darkness. We need to fight here. As Judith was sent by God to speak directly to the leader, Holofernes, we must also be willing to be sent directly to the leader, satan, Lucifer, to reclaim what belongs to God. God is now gathering His army together to attack because New Age is deadly, and the people who are coming against it can suffer severe repercussions. Some people in our own community have tried to expose New Age for what it is, and they have suffered tremendous retaliation from the enemy. This retaliation is another proof of the high-powered spirits moving behind New Age.

I'd also like to share a couple other situations where intercession moves powerfully in spiritual warfare. This only happens when we are led by God to move in prayer. We never move out without the Lord. We wait. When God can trust us, when He knows we're going to obey Him, then He can use us. Even when our logic may tell us differently, He wants us to obey Him. So there can be a lot of testings as we learn to be intercessors. This, too, is part of our protection. God will not send us forth until He is sure that we are ready, and the only way we can be ready is if we are faithful, obedient intercessors.

One day I was in church, and I met a young man who happened to tell me his story. He was a high priest and wanted to get out of the occult. I listened to his story with the hairs on my arms standing up. The evil was so strong, right in the presence of the Blessed Sacrament. I didn't enter into ministry or do anything. I just left. I thought, "Oh, Lord, I wonder why You wanted me to hear this. This is extremely dangerous." About 30 minutes later my phone rang. It was another friend of mine who had no idea where I'd been that afternoon, and she said, "I just got a word from the Lord for you. I have no idea what it means." That's pretty much a sign of a true prophet, when they don't try to interpret their own prophetic word. I trust those kind. I said, "That's okay. Just give me the word, and I'll take it to the Lord. He'll let me know." She said, "He said to tell you, 'Have nothing to do with the person you met today.' " And I thought , "Oh, this is a true word from the Lord, maybe." I went to my spiritual director, told him about it, and my spiritual director said the same thing, "Stay away from it. It's dangerous. Until the Lord reveals what to do, have nothing to do with it."

That's what I did. I didn't pray about it. Actually I was very relieved. I thought, "When You're ready to move Lord, in whatever way, You'll let me know. And if you never let me know, that's fine. You'll let somebody else know." A whole year went by, a whole year, and one day when I was in my own private prayer time, all of a sudden it was like I was watching a movie. I saw this young man in an apartment somewhere, and the Lord said, "Give the command." I said, "What?" He said, "Give the command." As I gave the command for satan to go, I saw this immense snake, it was huge, start to come out of the top of the head of this person. It just kept coming out and coming out and coming out, almost like possession. As the snake came out, it dropped to the floor and started to coil around and around. It was enormous! It was moving slowly, and the Lord said, "Give the command again and tell it to hurry." I did, and when the tail left and the whole snake was out, instantly that snake became satan himself. Instantly St. Michael, who hadn't even been in this scene, was there between Lucifer and myself, and I never saw satan again.

I looked at this young man in my image—he was just deflated. He was empty, there was nothing there. Then the Lord said, "Start praying for him for the infilling of My love and nurturing so he can become full of life." So I did; that was easy! This was intercession *led by the Lord, step by step, in the Lord's timing,* and it was easy. Today that young man is a monk in the Catholic Church!!! So it is easy. But what isn't so easy sometimes is the retaliation that we can get from this kind of prayer. This is why the armor is so important to keep us protected. It is one thing to have the sword, to have the power, but to know how to use the sword and to use it effectively is another. Satan will strike back, and this is when the armor is so important. He will retaliate.

Satan had set a trap for me. There are ambushes so we have to be careful. We don't go into deliverance or spiritual warfare every time we see a need for it. It is not that difficult to remove evil spirits, but if it's not in God's timing, within His perfect will, it's dangerous. Our protection, our sole protection here, is our obedience to God. Being in God's perfect will places His canopy of protection over us. If God asks us to do something, then God is responsible for taking care of us, and He will. If we move out under our own power, our own authority, no matter how good it looks, the consequences can be very costly and very serious. It's dangerous ministry but it's for children. It's for children who know how to wait for orders before they proceed. It's that easy.

When I first got into this ministry, people started coming to me, wanting to be set free. I really didn't know what to do because my only experience at that time was from reading about other peoples' ministries who were having success. They were in teams, particularly women who were in a team with a priest. I didn't know of anyone involved in spiritual warfare without a priest working with them. We did not have a priest in Omaha who wanted to become involved, so I didn't know what to do. I called one of the experts in another state and asked her what she thought I should do. She said, "Be careful. It's dangerous. I wouldn't do it without a priest." So I went to the Lord and said, "Lord, I don't know what You're trying to tell me. You're sending these people to me. I'm being advised not to become involved without a priest, but there isn't a priest. What should I do?" He said, "You have Me. I'm a high priest." So that's how we started. The ideal is to have a priest involved because by their office as priest, they have a power that causes satan to back down immediately. This particular ministry was strictly accomplished through prayer. Jesus was there with me. St. Michael, too, thank goodness! Jesus said to Peter, "Simon, Simon! Remember that satan has asked for you, to sift you like wheat. But I have prayed for you that your faith may never fail" (Lk 22:31-32). We have an Intercessor, Jesus, who is always praying for us and protecting us as well.

Let me just share a couple other instances that involve spiritual warfare at a different level. It really doesn't make any difference what level it is, as long as we're being led by the Lord. Many times we don't know where we're even going when we are in prayer. We don't know if we're going to visit someone or something in this country, or if we're going to be in a different city or country.

When we were in Europe, we prayed every night for the Lord to speak and show us whatever He wanted us to pray for. Five of us were traveling through Europe for about seven weeks, and we were interceding a lot. One night the Lord gave an image of a bride without a head. A headless bride. So we asked the Lord, "What does this mean?" There was no response. We thought, "Well, when You're ready to let us know, You'll let us know. In the meantime, we'll just enjoy Rome!" So we did! The next morning we took off for St. Peter's. We were all dressed in traveling clothes, no identification at all that we were religious, no identification that we were intercessors. We were gazing into the crypt of St. Peter. I was by myself, just kind of lost in thought about Peter and the Church, and all of a sudden a tap came on my shoulder. It was an elderly gentleman with the most beautiful peasant-type face, a real pure, very beautiful, very kind face. He could speak some English. He said, "Will you please pray for my country?" I thought, "I wonder how he knows I'm an intercessor?" But I said, "I'd be happy to do that. What is your country?" He said, "Czechoslovakia." I said, "How would you like us to pray for Czechoslovakia?" He said, "She is a country cut off from her head. Pray for reunion with Rome." Because we had had that image of a headless bride the night before, we knew how to pray, and of course, Czechoslovakia is now reunited with Rome. So we never know what God's going to do.

A woman in a nearby parish had invited many prayer groups in Omaha to come for an all-night vigil at one of our churches. We were to pray that the drug situation wouldn't grow here and that the Lord would take care of it. We were happy to be part of this prayer vigil. Our hour was 4-5 a.m., and we all were there praising the Lord. We had our Bibles and, as always, were waiting for God to guide us and to teach us how to pray. We begin all prayer asking God to guide us and teach us how to pray. "Lord teach us to pray (Lk 11:1). In this situation, at this time, show us how to pray." All of a sudden, through different Scriptures that talked about praising and thanking God, we were being shown an ambush that would happen early in the morning. We began to

149

suspect that we weren't really there praying for Omaha like everybody else was or like everybody else thought we were doing. We spent the whole hour praising the Lord and following exactly what He was showing us in the Scriptures, and that was it! At five o'clock another group came, and we dispersed. About four hours later, a phone call came from California. Very early that same morning, the biggest drug bust ever took place. It was an ambush! Some woman saw some strange behavior and called the police. The police were there and caught them. It was tremendous. So God didn't even tell us the location of the ambush, but through our obedience to pray the prayer that He wanted us to pray, He was able to move. See, the battle is the Lord's, thank goodness! The results and the fruit of it are the Lord's also. It's all the Lord's.

I could go on and on about the ways that God leads us in warfare, but I'll close with one about the Gulf War. I'm sure everybody was praying for the Gulf War when it was happening. Sometimes we may wonder, "Well, how *do* we pray? How do we pray here?" It was just kind of mass confusion. Day after day on television, we would watch country after country sending in troops, these many tanks, these many men, and these many planes. It was overwhelming, and it was all happening so fast. So we asked the Lord, "How do You want us to pray for the Gulf War situation?" He gave us two different things. The first one was, "I want you to pray for Israel." Not for America; He was going to have other intercessors do that. He wanted us to pray for Israel. So we asked, "How do You want us to pray for Israel?" The Lord said, "Pray that Israel will not retaliate because Israel is going to get hit, and Israel in anger is going to want to retaliate. The enemy wants that. Stop that. Beg Me to have America be the peacemaker and stop it." And that's exactly what happened!

This was practically our whole prayer focus in the Gulf War. Then one day, I said to the Lord, "You know

150

everybody is sending in their troops. What do You think about that?" He showed me an image of all these dark angels, fallen angels, mobilizing over that whole area. I didn't see any of the angels of light, God's good angels, so I asked, "Where are Your angels?" He said, "Nobody's asking Me to send in My angels." I couldn't believe it! Of course we weren't asking Him either. We had never thought of it. So we asked, "Oh, please, send in Your angels, Lord!" That's where the real battle is—in the spirit realm. These were the forces moving behind the leadership and the different things in the countries. That's what happened: God sent in His angels and the war of course did not last very long after that. The main play was the "Hail Mary." I thought, "My, look at all the people that were involved in the intercession, right along with our Lady." Beautiful!

We pray only for what God wants us to pray for and when He wants it. It's powerful. Effective intercession is effective simply because it is what God wants to do. Once God reveals His heart and mind on a particular issue, asking is simple. That's all we do: ask, and then He does it. We can spend a lot of time asking for all sorts of things that we want God to do. We can spend a lot of time in prayer explaining everything to the Lord about what He should do or what's wrong with this person or this situation, as though God doesn't know, as if God needs to be educated! But, we're the ones who need to know. We need to know God's mind, God's heart, and God's plan. Just by the fact that God lets us know how He wants us to pray is a fulfillment of what He said to the prophet Amos, "I never do anything without first letting My servants know." (Am 3:7) So when He lets us know, He is saying, "Now ask Me. Pray without ceasing. I need you to be My voice here on the earth."

Sometimes it means asking Him to not let something happen. It depends what it is that He is showing us, but many times our prayer is, "Lord, please let this happen and do this and this and this." The prayers must come through

151

Jesus, and we are His Jesus. Together we are the Body of Jesus Christ. The Father works only through the Body on account of Jesus, who lives now within us. Jesus has the power at the right hand of the Father in this tremendous, powerful intercession and He is then the sword of the Spirit in action. Therefore, **"At every opportunity, pray in the Spirit, using prayers and petitions of every sort. Pray constantly and attentively for all in the holy company"** (Eph 6:18).

Chapter 9

The Footgear of Zeal

*"Stand fast, with . . . zeal to propagate
the gospel of peace as your footgear."*
Eph 6:14-15

If we are going to stand fast, we really need to have the right kind of footwear. Zeal is our footgear. It's what moves us and enables us to go where we might not normally go. For women who wear high heels, we might stand for a while, but I'm not sure how steady we'd stand over a period of time. When we think of standing fast, we're really thinking of taking a firm, solid stand. We're going to hold our ground. So our footgear is extremely important. We've got to be able to hold our ground. With the situation in the Church and world today, we're going to be called upon more and more to hold our ground and defend the Church and bring the gospel of peace.

Little did many of us ever realize that anything in the book of Revelation would ever have anything to do with us. We tend to think that Revelation pertains to some other generation. We never even used to read it because we couldn't understand it anyway. But now every single word has meaning, doesn't it? It's clear. It's anointed. There still may be a lot of mystery, but the book of Revelation is for our time. We're living as we know now in chapter twelve of the book of Revelation. We are going to have to defend the Church.

We may have seen the Catholic Church visibly represented at the Cairo Conference in 1994 on television. Did we ever think we'd ever see something like that? We used to read about the saints being persecuted like this, but it never took place within our lifetime. People have been canonized because they represented the Church and spoke out publicly in her defense during difficult times. Most of us have read encyclicals and documents, but to actually see Rome visibly represented at that conference, standing up defending the sanctity of life, made me feel proud to be a Catholic. It was our own country, the United States, that was one of life's main enemies. It's rather frightening. So there are confrontations that are coming, and we need to be prepared. What a wonderful privilege it is to be a part of this time in history.

So we have to "Stand fast, with. . .zeal to propagate the gospel of peace as your footgear" (Eph 6:14-15). It's the gospel of peace. We will find that every part of the armor relates also to a Beatitude. The footgear of zeal correlates with "Blest, too, the peacemakers; they shall be called children of God" (Mt 5:9). We are to bring peace wherever we go. We are to be these peacemakers with our footgear of zeal. See how important it is for us to be little! I hope that if you don't take anything else away from this book, you will remember that we are called to be children. We are called to be vulnerable, empty, and weak. When we are weak, then we are strong. We're called to become one with our Leader, the Lamb. This is the Office of Intercession: to unite with the Lamb. Jesus wants to continue His redemptive mission to take away the sin of the world in, with, and through us now. "Look! There is the Lamb of God who takes away the sin of the world" (Jn 1:29). This is the calling of an intercessor.

Where do we really see this sin being taken way in great power and effectiveness? We see it particularly on Calvary. One of the great powers of Calvary, the great powers of the Crucifix, will be worked through us, particularly if we allow ourselves to be one with the Crucified Jesus. We will have pain. We will have suffering. This is one of the great powers of Calvary, of the Cross. One of the great deceptions in our culture today is that we need to run from the Cross, to run from anything that is the least bit distasteful. We have so many ways to do that.

But it is in the Cross that the power and wisdom of God lie. The Cross is the power and wisdom of God. One of the reasons it is the power of God is because it's love at its best. There is nothing more powerful than love, nothing. Jesus said, "There is no greater love than this: to lay down one's life for one's friends" (Jn 15:13). It takes love power to go to the Cross, allow the Cross to come into our lives, accept it, and use it. It's redemptive, and it has power. Jesus said, "The Father loves me for this: that I lay down my life to take it up again. No one takes it from me; *I lay it down freely*. I have power to lay it down, and I have power to take it up again" (Jn 10:17-18). Most of us may not want to use that kind of power if it means we are to lay down our lives. Maybe we can't. Maybe we don't have that level of love to lay our lives down. That takes agape love, sacrificial love. That's the Lamb of God love. It's all right if we don't have that kind of love yet, but how can we get it? We can ask for it. We can ask for that kind of love.

In Lent we celebrate the Passion of Jesus. The Passion of Jesus is this kind of love; it's a passionate love. The Church needs lovers today, passionate lovers, with a wild, reckless, passionate love, intense, extreme, and radical. If we want to be radical, we should be radical in our love.

After the Resurrection, Jesus asked Peter, "Simon, son of John, do you love Me?" Jesus was using the Greek word *filio*, which refers to that beautiful friendship love, family

155

love, brotherly-sisterly love. "Do you *filio* Me, Peter?" Peter replied, "Yes, Lord, you know that I love (filio) You." Then Jesus asked him again. Peter is getting more distressed about it and said, "Yes, Lord. You know that I love (filio) You." When Jesus asked, "Simon, son of John, do you love me?" the third time, He changed the meaning of the word love to "agape" this time. "Peter, do you agape Me?" In other words, "Do you love Me with a love that's a Calvary love? Do you love Me with a love that will lay down your life for Me?" Peter was grieved, and His reply was, "Lord, you know all things and You know that I filio You" (Jn 21:15-17).

Peter had learned humility by now. He had learned to speak truth, and he had learned who he was. He didn't have that kind of love yet, and he could honestly admit it. But the question was, "Do you love Me with agape love? Do you love Me more than these?" (Jn 21:17) Agape love is that "more" love. It's going the extra mile in your brother's shoes, and it's costly. It can cost us our lives. It can cost us our lives without our physical death. It can cost us our reputation, our friends, or for some of us, our jobs.

I had a friend who worked for a very large contracting firm here in Omaha. He had just received a new infilling through the Baptism of the Holy Spirit, and he was bursting in love with the Lord. Now the Holy Spirit was calling him to this very pure, radical type of love. He was very distressed about it because he was very high up in the executive area of his firm, and the way they got these big contracting jobs was that they padded the accounts. The bids were not quite true. So he said, "If I don't pad these bids and change them, I'll lose my job." I asked him, "If you don't stop doing that, what's your option?" "I'm afraid I'll lose the Lord." He said, "I don't know what to do." I said, "I think you have your answer." He said, "I think I do, too, but I needed to hear it." I said, "You always have to choose truth. You have to choose what's right. You have to look at the fact that you'll lose your job, but God will never let you down when you do what He wants and what is right." So that's what he did. He was responsible for a wife and seven children so this was a big decision. So he told them he couldn't pad the accounts any more, he couldn't lie, and they fired him. Very shortly after that, the Lord showed him how to start his own firm.

The Lord will stand by us, but it takes that kind of love. It takes a love greater than our own love. It isn't that we don't love God, but it's that sometimes we don't love God more than we love ourselves. That's the problem. The choice usually isn't between satan and God's kingdoms. It's within our little kingdom of ourselves. Who do we love the most? This is oftentimes the choice we have to make, and this choice can lead us to Calvary if it's the right choice. This is zeal at its best: if we can lay down our lives for our friends. Who are our friends? They are God's friends. Whoever His friends are become our friends.

One time I was reading an interview with John Kennedy, and the question was, "Jacqueline must love politics." Obviously she wouldn't have married a politician if that wasn't her number one interest. He said, "Oh, no. Quite the contrary. She doesn't care for politics at all." "Oh. Then how does this work?" He said, "It's easy. I'm committed to politics, Jacqueline's committed to me, and therefore, she is committed to politics." I heard that and thought, "Lord, I think You're talking to me. I'm not really committed to the Cross, but I'm committed to God. You love that Cross, and You love all these people, so I'm committed to them, too."

"In His own flesh He abolished the law with its commands and precepts, to create in Himself one new man from us who had been two and to make peace, reconciling both of us to God in One Body through His Cross" (Eph 2:15-16). Paul was called to this tremendous ministry of reconciliation, to stand in the gap, to connect man and God. Have you ever wondered where the gap is? Sometimes we think we're going to bridge something, but where the gap

157

really is, is between heaven and earth, between God and man. So to "bridge the gap" means we go on the Cross. It is the Cross, that suffering or pain, that we have willingly accepted on behalf of the Body of Christ that bridges the gap. The Cross is where God and man touch and are reconciled. So Jesus returns now in the Power of His Spirit to relive this beautiful expression of love again and again through us. We live in a perpetual state of total surrender, total passivity, total victimhood. Jesus desires to lay down His life in those of us who will consent to be His victim lambs, victim lambs in the good sense of redemption and love. "Let it be done to me as you say" (Lk 1:38). It's just that simple. The Spirit will take us to the cross that is perfect for us if we will but consent to be used.

If somebody says to us, or when we say, "I love you," there really isn't anything more to say. Those three words are the epitome. What else can we really say except to say it again and again and again. When Jesus was on the Cross, this is what He was saying to the Father and to the world: I love you. This is what Jesus wants to say over and over again, but this time, through us and our sacrifices. This agape love is the weapon of all weapons that will take away the sin, and thereby conquer the evil. This Calvary love, dying to my own desires so that someone else may live, is the best expression of love. It is the fullest expression of obedience, submission, and surrender to God's plan.

When I talk about the Cross being the power and the wisdom of God, I don't think that I've fully understood wisdom. I would get little glimpses. I would read about it. I was at the stage where part of the gift of Wisdom, which we all received at Confirmation, was beginning to be activated. I was beginning to see what God sees, beginning to have a different viewpoint, and beginning to be able to enter more fully into the mind and heart of God. That's very much what the gift of Wisdom does.

When I came home from the cloister, the Lord had me travel around to see some of the new religious order and movements that were going on in the Church for about a year. I began meeting different foundresses and founders for the first time and hearing about their journeys and their calls. They all were so well formed by God, trained and intelligent. They really seemed to know what they were doing. Many had a few different degrees, and they were well prepared. I was taking all this in subconsciously until finally the last order I visited was just too much. My psyche couldn't handle the overload anymore. I wasn't dealing with it, and I developed a terrible headache that lasted for three days. God was stopping me to make me take a look at the things I was stuffing. I was worried, so I prayed, "They are so intelligent. They're so well prepared. They're so knowledgeable. They're so educated. Lord, I just kind of wonder if You've made a mistake here. What am I doing out here?" I was beginning to feel that I didn't know anything because I really didn't, so I started asking God for wisdom. "What is wisdom, Lord? I need it and I need it now." Usually He doesn't give me Scriptures outright, but He did this time because I was so desperately in need of a Scripture. He said, "I will give you a Scripture on Wisdom." I said, "Oh, thank goodness. I'll have this wisdom, and I'll be okay." He gave me Isaiah 53; it's all about the Suffering Servant. "Like a lamb led to the slaughter . . . he was silent and opened not his mouth" (Is 53:7). I couldn't believe it!

But this is wisdom: being led to the slaughter is wisdom at its best because it's Calvary love. It's Lamb of God love, vulnerability, helplessness, weakness, victimhood, silence. We want to defend ourselves all the time, but "If he gives his life as an offering for sin, he shall see his descendants in a long life and the will of the Lord shall be accomplished through him" (Is 53:10). That's wisdom: to be used by the Lord so that He can accomplish what He desires through us.

Then I turned to the Wisdom literature in the Bible. It's very beautiful to pray through, and this is when I began to notice that the pronoun changes in the Wisdom literature to "she." Everything is she in reference to wisdom. Everything else in the Bible about God and about the things of God is referred to as "he." But in the Book of Wisdom, the Spirit of Wisdom is referred to as she. So I asked about that and the reply was, "The highest form of wisdom is surrender. It's in the feminine part of us that we surrender." The Church is Bride. The soul is feminine. We have to perpetually wave that little white flag of surrender, and if we can't surrender, at least we don't run. That's the main thing: don't run! I can say, "Don't run!" from one who has spent a great deal of time running. One way I used to run a lot was long telephone conversations. I would talk on the phone to avoid talking it over with God. That was my escape. I don't do that anymore, and it's wonderful not to run.

We have many different ways to run from pain and from something we don't want to confront, particularly in ourselves. This is where the footgear of zeal comes in. Zeal runs *toward* Calvary, not away. Zeal runs with that tremendous love so that souls can come home and be reconciled and reunited with the Father. "Zeal for your house consumes me" (Jn 2:17). This was the attitude the disciples witnessed in Jesus. It completely consumed Him. That's the kind of zeal that we want: that we will have so much love that it will just consume us, that it will take over as a burning fire from within. We need to come to know the Father so well that we will want the whole world to also know the Father. For in this our joy, too, will be complete.

It's not enough for us just to love God and to be loved by God. We want others to have this experience. Jesus said, "Eternal life is this: to know You, the one true God . . ." (Jn 17:3). That means to experience Him, to know Him. We want to obtain this gift of eternal life now. We're going to know the Father, Jesus, the Holy Spirit, all the angels and saints, friends, families for all eternity, but the gift of eternal life can begin now. We can know the Father now. We can free souls now that are in captivity, in bondage, and in darkness through our sacrifice. They need the Father. They need Jesus. They need to be in light. They need to be set free. We do this with the weapon of the Cross—the weapon of Love!

Satan harassed Jesus throughout His life, but the fruit this harassment brought forth changed the world forever! We hear the authority Jesus takes, we witness the healings, and we see the beautiful deliverance ministry develop. We see the beautiful ministry of the Lord. When Jesus is actually on the Cross, it's almost like satan begins to realize that he just made the biggest mistake he could have made. Everything satan did was to try to get Jesus killed. He stirred up the crowds and the leaders in an attempt to get Jesus crucified. Now it looked like he had succeeded. Jesus is hanging on the Cross. He is dying, and it's like somehow the light came to satan that he had made his worst mistake for all eternity. So now comes his last shot of harassment to stop the power of the Cross, "Come down off that cross if You are God's Son!" (Mt 27:40)

That's the temptation: to run from the very thing that will bring forth life. When we are in pain and are having our reputations battered, it's hard to remember that the Cross is victory. When we don't feel good, and we're wearing the crown of thorns or whatever that suffering may be, we're going to hear these same words from satan, "Walk away from it. You don't have to take this." As he enticed Jesus, "Come down off that Cross" (Mk 15:32), satan will try to dissuade us from this redemptive work. This is when we have to be careful.

This temptation to run is the last tool satan uses to turn us back from the triumph of the Cross, and it's powerful. It's powerful because it hits us when we're most vulnerable. Maybe we haven't had any prayer experiences for a while or our prayer has been pretty dry for a long time. Most of us can take something for a short time, but maybe this empty dry spell has gone on for a long time. "How long, O Lord? Will You utterly forget me? How long will You hide your face from me?" (Ps 13:2) The Psalmist has a beautiful psalm, "How long, O Lord! How long?" We can start to put a time frame on "how long" because we almost unconsciously have our own agenda. We forget to stay focused on the why and the Who we are doing things for. "I'll do this for such and such a period of time," but after a week of it, "How long does this have to continue, Lord? How long?" So always be careful of the temptation to turn back.

When we are in this Calvary position, when we willingly accept pain and suffering for the Body of Christ, the battle is fierce. Suffering comes particularly on three levels: emotional, physical, and spiritual. Suffering of any kind leaves us vulnerable and weak. Suffering is difficult, but we don't have to be ashamed of it. We can choose to unite our suffering with Jesus, the Lamb.

The gifts of faith, hope, and love are so important because they keep us in this union. We know that we're going to make the passover. Hope carries us to the Resurrection. We know that there will be light at the end of the tunnel. We know we're going to have the victory. We know we're in the perfect will of God. So no matter how difficult it's going to be, when we're firmly anchored, in union with God, deep within there is peace. "God's own peace, which is beyond all understanding, will stand guard over your hearts . . ." (Phil 4:7). Satan cannot rob us of that. There is a whole area within us where no one can go except us and the Lord, and we're safe there. Our faith will not leave us, hope will not leave us, and love will not leave us because we're united with our Leader. It's our union with Jesus that will strengthen our faith, hope, and love.

When we're united with Jesus in a special way, we're united with Wisdom Incarnate. Wisdom is now enfleshed within us, and it starts taking over. This is why Paul could say these beautiful words, "In my own flesh I fill up what is lacking in the suffering of Christ for the sake of His Body, the Church" (Col 1:24). That's zeal. We're not allowing this or doing this for ourselves. We're being used by God. What's lacking in the sufferings of Christ? Jesus has won all the graces, but they need to be distributed now, and He does it through His Body. Redemption takes place with flesh and blood, with the Spirit moving within these human temples. Do you see now why the Cross is the wisdom and the power of God? There's nothing more powerful because this is love at its best.

When I was in the novitiate, a priest told me that his mother was dying. We felt very badly about that, and his reply was, "It's all right. She's in pain, but what's beautiful is it's not wasted pain." He felt the greatest tragedy in the world isn't pain, but it's wasted pain. Pain in itself isn't good, but when our pain is united with the sufferings of the Lord and offered for others, it can bring forth much fruit. At Pentecost we see the tremendous blessing and love of God coming upon His people. There's a cost to Pentecost and when we want these graces for our Church, our nation, our loved ones, and our families, then we must be willing to pay that price as did the few people who remained with Jesus at the foot of the Cross. Zeal is this willingness to be used by God in whatever way He sees fit to win souls to Him. We stand at the foot of the Cross along with Our Lady of Sorrows, the Beloved John, and Mary Magdalene. They stood there. They were Jesus' friends, and they also suffered.

I have wondered who suffered the most—Jesus or Mary? Some of us would much rather have the suffering ourselves than watch a loved one suffer or die. I don't think there's any suffering as great as that myself. The suffering of Our Lady and of those who have watched loved ones die is incredible. There are no words for it. There's no pain like it, but Mary had that prophetic word herself from Simeon, "And you yourself shall be pierced with a sword so that the thoughts of many hearts may be laid bare" (Lk 2:35). Being willing to allow the sword to pierce your own heart for others is so important. If pain is piercing your heart, know it's redemptive. It *is* achieving the end to which it started; heart thoughts will be laid bare. During the pain or the suffering, pray for the graces to endure. Pray for the graces for whoever or whatever in the Body of Christ needs the extra graces and healing.

Many times we can intercede, but we may not see anything happening. Then pain will come. It can be pain from a friend who spoke unkindly. It can be pain from the death of a loved one. It can be the pain of animals we love that are dying. But it's pain, and when that pain comes, we can be pretty sure we've gotten a tremendous breakthrough somehow, somewhere, for someone we've been praying for. Sometimes God will let us know who our pain or suffering helped in order to give us the courage and faith to keep going.

What about pain of fasting? This pain of denial of food can be redemptive, but only if the Lord wants it. I came from a lifestyle of fasting, as cloistered people do a lot of fasting. It's part of the lifestyle and rule, and yet I had a very difficult time fasting those first two or three months after I came home from the cloister. I began to get headaches and was tired, so the Lord showed me in order to fast well, I had to eat well. I had to eat correctly on all the other days, or else when the days of fast would come, I wouldn't have that energy to carry me. At this time I wasn't eating right. I'd just grab a cheese sandwich everyday, and eat it in the car on the run. So when it came to fasting I didn't have the vitamins or the energy, and I was getting rundown. Preparing ourselves for our fast days by eating well on the non-fast days makes sense. Fasting is scriptural and can bring power to our intercession if the Father wants it.

Mary at Medjugorje is asking people to fast on bread and water. We've been to Medjugorje many times, but we always have to ask God about everything, even messages from heaven. When I asked if that particular fast of bread and water would be all right for me to do, I received my answer from Our Lady, "No." I asked, "Then what kind of a fast would you want from me?" She said, "I want you to eat right." Fasting wouldn't be that difficult for me, but Mary wanted me to have high energy. The eight-day fast that I did on my own caused me to practically collapse by the fourth day. This was because this type of fast was something *I* wanted to do. This wasn't what God was asking me to do, so I didn't have the necessary graces.

When I first came home from the cloister, the Lord asked me to fast the entire Lent. I thought I was hearing things because I hadn't done well with it before, but He wanted it. He wanted a fast strictly on fruit juice. When I told this to a doctor friend of mine, he said, "I don't like the idea. What does your spiritual director say?" "He said it's okay, but I'm supposed to check it out with you." The doctor said, "Let's see what happens after ten or fifteen days of the fast, halfway through Lent, then I'm going to check your blood and see how you're doing." I said, "Okay. That's fair enough." So halfway through Lent, I went into his office and had my blood checked. He couldn't believe it! I don't know anything about blood but my hemoglobin was 14.9. Fifteen was supposed to be really good. I was in excellent health. I never felt better in my life! Easiest thing I ever did. I found out I needed very little sleep, so I had lots and lots of time to pray. It was wonderful, but this was because of the grace of God for those forty days. He has never asked me for this type of fast since. Fasting can be redemptive, but it must be the Lord initiating the fast if it is to bear fruit.

There is tremendous power in fasting. When we fast more than a day, we find our body will start to release poisons. Maybe you've discovered this. Medical people already know this, but I made that discovery and thought, "Oh, isn't this interesting?" There's a healing that starts to take place in our bodies, and energies and all sorts of wonderful things start to happen in fasting. The Lord showed me that the cleansing and energizing that happens within our bodies during fasting works the same way in the Mystical Body of Christ. Our fasting carries the cleansing and deliverance power to cast out the poison in His Mystical Body, the Church. It can cast out the spiritual poison throughout His entire Body. It carries the energizing power to set souls on fire with love for God. What happens in our physical body during fasting can happen throughout the Mystical Body through fasting. It's so powerful.

So pain can come through fasting. Have you noticed all the temptations that suddenly come on fast days? We might not think of food all week long and then all of a sudden, it's a fast day, and we're hungry for breakfast right away. Fasting can be sacrificial because it's our will that is being sacrificed. This is our gift: to lay aside our own preferences and wants to allow this cleansing and energizing to take place within the Body. Our free will is the only gift we really have to give. We place our free will on the altar, particularly the altar within our heart, in union with the Lamb. We are willing to become sacrificial lambs. That's our gift. The Father gave us the beautiful gift of our free will. The most precious gift we have is our ability to keep offering it back to Him. So it's a sacrifice of love. It's a sacrifice of praise and the fruit of it is tremendous joy. It's tremendous joy that God can have His way with us and out of all this sacrifice comes that phenomenal peace.

I remember when we were praying so hard for a friend of mine who had severe headaches in addition to several other things wrong. She was on total disability. Neurologists, psychiatrists, and all kinds of other doctors had looked at her and tested her for a long period of time. Finally she went to Boston and underwent more grueling tests on the brain, back, and spine. They absolutely couldn't find what was really wrong. She was not getting the help from the medical profession so we were all praying and praying for the Lord to heal her.

She wasn't too far from Fr. DiOrio's place. I said, "Why don't you hop in a car and go up there and have him pray over you? What have you got to lose?" She said, "Well, I'll try, but I don't know if I can. I'll have to have somebody take me." She was really quite sick but nobody could take her at the appointed time. In the meantime, we were pulling together a big conference in Omaha. We were all busy and tired, and the day before the conference, my cat was killed. We all loved this cat, and even a doctor friend of mine who hated cats cried because she was a very special cat. Now I really felt this deep pain. I was so tired from all the preparations and work that I didn't have those extra resources within myself to get my equilibrium back. But what came to my mind right away was my friend. I prayed, "Lord, use this pain. It might just be a little pain to somebody else, but my heart is pierced right now over something that I loved very deeply that has just been killed. Use it for my friend, Lord, and heal her." And He did; she was healed! I think she could have flown home without the airplane! So pain isn't bad in itself if we unite it with the pierced heart of Jesus.

Whatever the retreat, whether it lasts three days or thirty days, St. Ignatius always wants the retreatant to contemplate God's deep love for them on the last day of the retreat. It's part of the spiritual exercises of St. Ignatius to strengthen us. I was on a thirty-day discernment retreat and was in the balcony of the chapel on the last day of my retreat. I was gazing at this immense crucifix. All of a sudden, it was like that crucifix came alive, and Jesus was alive on it. Then I saw the piercing of His heart, with that water and blood flowing out. In the image there was an altar with seven huge chalices catching the blood and water. The Lord showed me that these seven chalices are the sacramental system of the

Church. The sacraments are life, but where does that life come from? Where's the source? The life is being poured forth from the heart of Jesus. It was through Jesus' sacrifice of His very life that He brought life to the whole Church. When we go on the Cross with Jesus and let our hearts be pierced, we, too, are giving life to the Church. It's mystical, but it's real. We are life bearers, life givers. This is why Jesus came—to bring life. Jesus said, "I came that they might have life and have it to the full" (Jn 10:10).

So once again, we go back to that beautiful Beatitude, "Blessed are the peacemakers" (Mt 5:9). This is the gospel of peace to empower us to reconcile man with God again, to bring life back into people and into the Catholic Church. The Church does not have the spiritual life and vitality flowing through her that she needs right now. People may be at Mass in a physical sense, but maybe not spiritually. They are thirsty and hungry. And so the call comes, "Will you offer up your very life for My people? Will you willingly choose to be vulnerable and appear foolish in the eyes of the world? Will you allow Me full control of you and your life?"

Have you ever noticed how we try to reconcile with each other? We'll say, "Well, I'm sorry" but the way we do this means that we still have the control. We're saying to someone, "I'm sorry. Now if you don't want to accept that, that's not my problem. I'm going to wash my hands and walk away because I have apologized." We can get full of pride that way. "I'm so big hearted that I made this big step and apologized." Apologizing is wonderful but the Lord showed me that's not the way He wants me to apologize. "Say you're sorry, but take the next step and let go of the control, and ask, 'Can you forgive me or will you forgive me?'" When I do this, I am vulnerable. My freedom and my acceptance is up to them. I'm at their mercy. I am the victim lamb again. God is calling us to this kind of vulnerability, to let His peace and love flow even if it means my feelings might get hurt. It's a step by step process, one little step after another.

"Blest are the peacemakers, they shall be called children of God" (Mt 5:9). This is a ministry of reconciliation, of making peace, of bringing God's life when it has gone by the wayside. It's a ministry for children. Children don't count the cost of love; they just do it. We are all children of God, and we're blessed because of it. Joy wells up as we go forth and love in Jesus' name. There is a happiness if we have this kind of "be happy" attitude.

If we are going to stand fast, we really need to have the right kind of footwear. Zeal for the salvation of souls is our footgear. It's what moves us, it's what enables us to go where we might not normally go. So **Stand fast, with . . . zeal to propagate the gospel of peace as your footgear"** (Eph 6:14-15).

Epilogue

"Draw your strength
from the Lord and his mighty power.
Put on the armor of God so that you may be able to stand
firm against the tactics of the devil."
Eph 6:10-11

Draw your strength from the Lord. It takes strength, but not our strength. I love the song, "The Joy of the Lord is My Strength." Joy is a fruit of God's Presence, His infallible Presence. We can count on it. Satan cannot counterfeit joy, so it is our strength. We have the inner joy of the Spirit, the fruit of union, the fruit of God's union. It's the great fruit of Pentecost, that beautiful intoxication of love, joy, and new wine. So draw your strength from the Lord and His mighty power.

When we were confirmed as soldiers of Christ and commissioned to fight the good fight, we received the armor of God through the sevenfold gifts of the Holy Spirit for this purpose. However, it is in our daily yes to the overshadowing of His Presence and our daily surrender to the action of His gifts that we put on the armor of God and are clothed with power from on High!

1. **Fortitude** enables us to draw strength from the Lord and His mighty power by giving us courage to meet the unseen foe in the daily trials and tribulations of suffering love, knowing that He is with us always.

2. **Fear of the Lord** enables us to put on the breastplate of justice, righteousness, and sinlessness through a deep hatred for sin and choosing to do only what pleases the Father. It sets us apart to go forth into battle with the Woman clothed with the Sun, to make war upon the serpent with her holy offspring, Jesus.

3. **Knowledge** enables us to put on the helmet of salvation and have the mind of Jesus Christ, thereby entering into His sonship and into our true identity as children of God. In this posture of humility and mindset of total dependency, we indeed enter into the victory of the Lamb.

4. **Counsel** enables us to stand fast with truth as our belt for who has known the mind and heart of God except the Holy Spirit? With this discerning light, the hidden counsels of God reveal the deepest deceptions of enemy bondage and the ultimate freedom of God's power.

5. **Piety** equips us with the footgear of zeal to propagate the gospel of peace. This reconciliation empowerment enables us to lay down our lives for our brothers and sisters. As blessed peacemakers, we, in union with Jesus, defeat the enemy by the Blood of the Lamb for the greater honor and glory of the Father.

6. **Understanding** is the shield of faith that enlightens the eyes of the heart to see. The fiery darts of the enemy are extinguished by the insight of a prayer warrior who assents to the truth that all things are possible with God.

7. **Wisdom** enables us to put on the Lord Jesus Christ. Transformed into the Word of God (Rv 19:13), the Holy Spirit uses us as His sword to engage in the battle, "not against human forces but against the principalities and

powers, the rulers of this world of darkness and the evil spirits in regions above" (Eph 6:12). "They will fight against the Lamb, but the Lamb will conquer them, for He is the Lord of lords and the King of kings; victorious, too, will be His followers—the ones who were called the chosen and faithful (Rv 17:14).

The battle belongs to the Lord, but it's done by the Lord through children, "with a little child to guide them" (Is 11:6). Our Commander-in-Chief is a child. He chooses to remain a child in us and bring us into that beautiful spirit of childhood within so that we continually cry out in total dependence, "Daddy, Abba, Father."

I'd like to share an image that the Lord gave me on Pentecost Sunday. I'd not been home from the cloister very long, so God was very busy teaching me things. Not that He isn't busy teaching me now! We are always in the process of learning. All the charismatics were gathering for Pentecost Mass, and as we were driving one of the women said, "Oh, did you see that snake?" I said, "No, I didn't, thank goodness!" This is amazing that I'm in deliverance ministry because I can't even stand a worm! I was the only one in the cloister who had permission to wear garden gloves in case I would touch a worm while gardening! She said, "It was strange because instead of lying along the highway, it was coiled up like it was going to strike."

That was all that was said. We went on to the Church. Before Mass, Father said, "If anybody has a special intention, put it especially on the altar and see what the Lord wants us to do. God really wants us to have very special intentions for this Mass." I was missing my community in the cloister, so my intention was community. I really wanted community.

After receiving our Lord in Communion, I went back and knelt down. It was like I was seeing a movie. It's something I'll never forget. It began with the recall of the friend sharing about that snake which I did not see. Now in

172

imagery I was seeing the snake, and it's ready to strike. It's going to strike straight up, and it's going to strike at me. Right then, the Lord lifted me up and showed me that it was getting ready to strike at my heel. It was so much like the Scripture in Genesis (Ch 3). So I was watching this and saw myself go up. The next thing I saw was someone kneeling in front of the Father. They looked like Joan of Arc. I could only see from the back, but this person was receiving the armor. It wasn't until a few minutes later when the person turned around that I realized it was myself!

This is the first thing God wanted me to know. We talk very casually about the armor of God and putting on the armor of God, but *we* don't put it on. It's *God's* armor, and *He* puts it on us. It's very much an interior armor. It's not something exterior; it's more interior.

The image continued. I'm very, very little and am in this armor. I thought, "I wonder what's going to happen now." The next thing I knew, I was picked up by the Lord and set on this beautiful white horse. He's on it, too. It was like when we have a little child sit in front of the rider. I was real little in this armor, looking absolutely ridiculous, but the Lord was there on this beautiful white horse, and all of a sudden—silence! When silence comes, it can sometimes get our attention more than words. I was becoming aware of the silence, and sitting on the horse, I could hear a very soft and gentle pawing rhythm. I turned around and saw a whole army of others on white horses. The horses were just pawing gently, waiting very obediently.

I looked ahead and wondered, "Why are we all lined up here?" All of a sudden the image opened up and across from me, maybe the length of a swimming pool, was another army with all black horses, and satan was there as their leader. We were face to face, and I thought, "There's going to be a tremendous confrontation here." In the satanic army they had spears that were like burning arrows. I thought, "Oh my, they're going to throw those over here at us any moment now. We don't have that kind of fire. Where is our fire?" All of a sudden I looked around again, and I saw these burning flames inside everyone. I looked down within myself and saw the same. We all had the fire of the Holy Spirit burning within us. We had God's Love, God's Spirit, God's Fire.

Everyone was looking to the Father for the signal. Nobody was moving, and I realized the Father is in total control. He's got the whole world in His hands, and He's got satan in His hands, too. He's got all of us. He is in control. He is the One to deliver us from this evil. He will give the signal to this army with Jesus at the head, and along with St. Michael, we'll go forth.

We are being prepared. We are being clothed in the armor that we need for this battle that is coming. This is an armor given to us by God. Let God put this armor on you. It's all gift. It's grace. We can ask and then be able to receive. This is an armor given to us by God; we can't take it off or put it on. We *become* the armor.

Concluding Prayer

ORANTE

Confer, O Lord, on us, who stand with Mary at the foot of the Cross, that union with You and trust in her, to which it is given to conquer the world. Help us to put on the armor of God: to battle, not against human forces, but against the principalities and powers, the rulers of this world of darkness, the evil spirits in regions above. Help us to stand fast, with truth as the belt around our waist, justice as our breastplate, and zeal to propagate the gospel of peace as our footgear.

Grant us that fullness of faith, firm and immovable as a rock, through which we shall rest tranquil and steadfast amid the crosses, toils, and disappointments of life; a courageous faith which will inspire us to undertake and carry out without hesitation great things for God and for the salvation of souls; a faith which will lead us forth united, to enkindle everywhere the fires of Divine Love, to enlighten those who are in darkness and in the shadow of death - to inflame those who are lukewarm - to bring back life to those who are dead in sin and a faith which will in all circumstances be our shield to extinguish the fiery darts of the evil one.

Teach us to have the Your mind, to wear the helmet of salvation and to become the sword of the Spirit, the Word of God. Make us aware to pray at every opportunity in the Spirit, especially for all in the holy company. Bless all those who have washed their robes and made them white in Your Blood with the gift of life-giving water, so that when the battle of life is over, all praise, honor, glory, and thanksgiving may be given to the One seated on the throne and to You, the Lamb who was slain, forever and ever. Amen.

Intercessors of the Lamb

The Intercessors of the Lamb is a mixed community of Priests, Brothers, Sisters and Laity who have been called to discipleship by the Holy Spirit and formed in the Heart of Mary to continue the redemptive mission of the Lamb of God through His powerful "burden-bearing" ministry of intercession. Committed to live Jesus and His Cross for the purpose of taking away the sin of the world, equipped with tools for spiritual warfare and in the power of the Holy Spirit, we are commissioned to the powerful ministry of intercession which springs forth from the wellspring of Divine Love flowing from the pierced Heart of Jesus. In union with the Lamb who was slain, we advance and establish the Kingdom of God **within**, thus preparing the Bride for the contemplative union of Love. Our goal is to develop and foster a deep interior life in the hearts of God's people so that they might become, within themselves, "a house of prayer" (Is 56:7) as God is within Himself. Because it is the life that prays, our own personal relationship with Jesus is the root and power of all effective intercession. The stronger our union with His Heart, the more our hearts begin to beat like His…a steady, slow beat…a beat that always says, "Souls…souls…souls." Striving to cast Fire upon the earth to make all things new, we show forth the mystery of God's merciful Love to the praise and glory of His Name! Those among the people of God particularly entrusted to this Apostolate are the Shepherds of the flock to whom we commit ourselves to support through the witness of our lives and the power of prayer.

Intercessors of the Lamb
4014 North Post Road, Omaha, NE 68112-1263
Phone: 402-455-5262, Fax: 402-455-1323
E-mail: bellwether@novia.net, Web: www.bellwetheromaha.org